Copyright © 2020 Brain Trainer All rights reserved.

No part of this publication may be reproduced, distributed or transmitted in any form or by any means, including photocopying, recording, or other electronic or mechanical methods, without the prior written permission of the publisher, except in the case of brief quotations embodied in critical reviews and certain other non-commercial uses permitted by copyright law.

Trademarked names appear throughout this book. Rather than use a trademark symbol with every occurrence of a trademarked name, names are used in an editorial fashion, with no intention of infringement of the respective owner's trademark. The information in this book is distributed on an "as is" basis, without warranty. Although every precaution has been taken in the preparation of this work, neither the author nor the publisher shall have any liability to any person or entity with respect to any loss or damage caused or alleged to be caused directly or indirectly by the information contained in this book.

Target Puzzle Guide

The goal of a Nine Letter Target Puzzle is to find as many words as possible by joining letters. An extra challenge is to find the hidden '9 letter word' that is made up of every letter in the puzzle!

There are certain rules a player must abide by.

(1) The Center letter MUST be used in every word:
e.g In the example puzzle above 'REAL', 'LEAN', 'TREE' are all valid words, whereas 'RANT' is invalid as it doesnt use the required center letter 'E'.

(2) A Letter can only be used once:
e.g In the example puzzle above 'TREE' is valid as there are two 'E' letters available to use, however 'RARE' is invalid as there is only one 'R' in the puzzle.

Important Notes:
 - Letters are not required to be next to the previous letter e.g 'LANE' is a valid word in the puzzle above despite the 'A' not being next to the 'L'
 - These puzzles are designed to be hard and very few people can reach 'Excellent' level.

Vocabulary Exercise:
 - Expect to come across many words in the solutions that aren't used in every day conversations. We advise that every time you complete a puzzle, check the answers at the back of the book and look up words that you aren't familar with. In this way not only are you keeping your mind active, but you get the added benefit of an increased vocabulary!

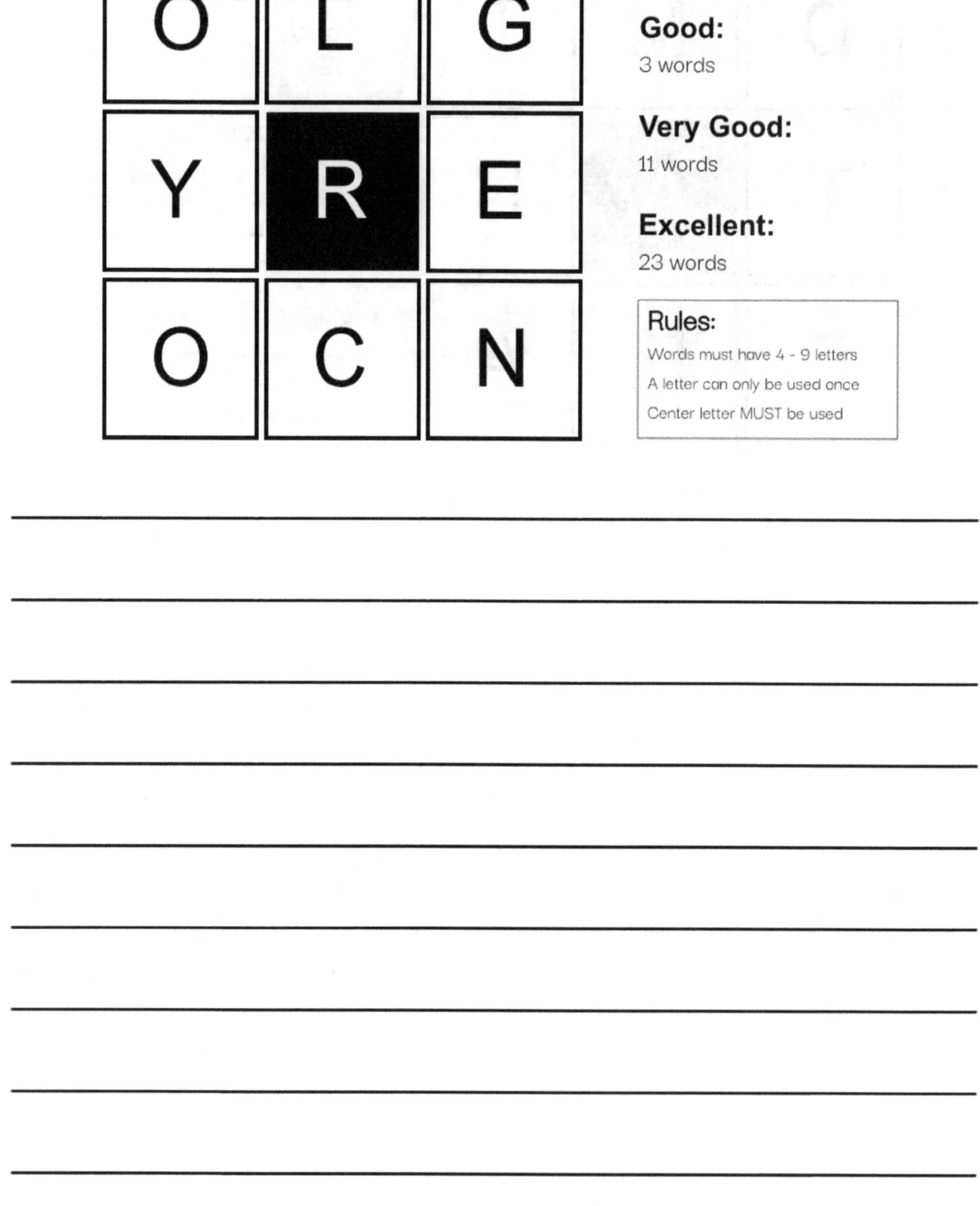

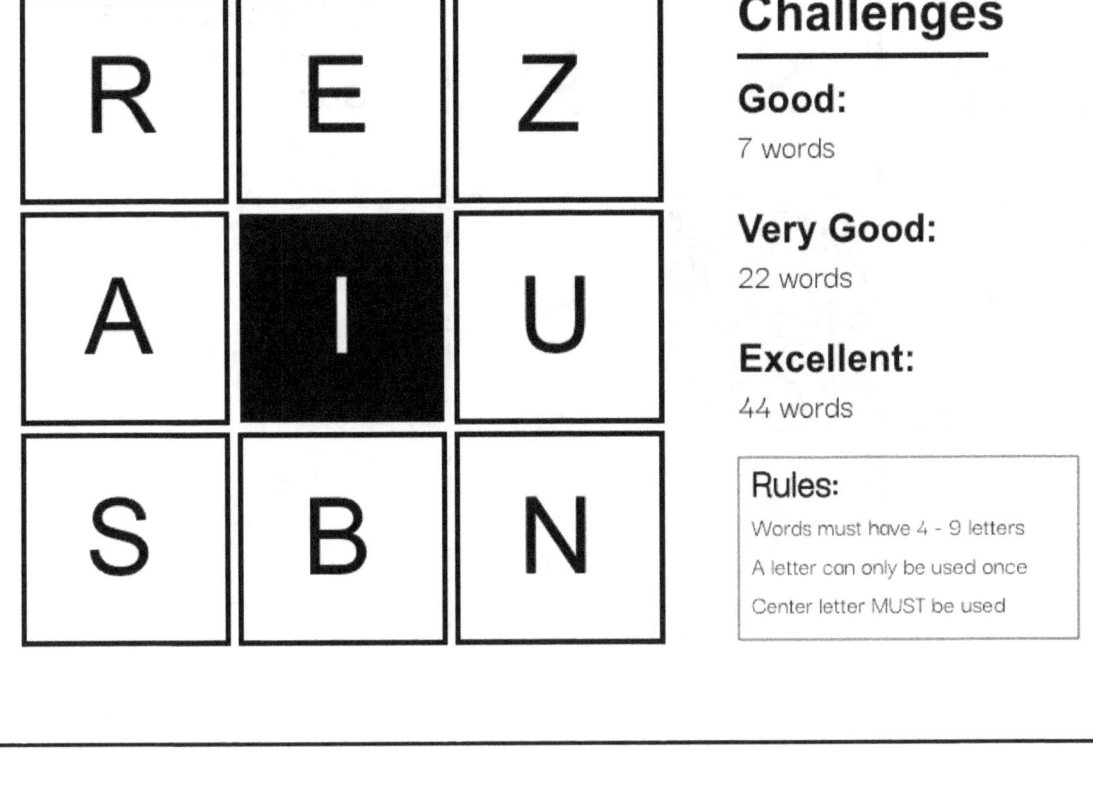

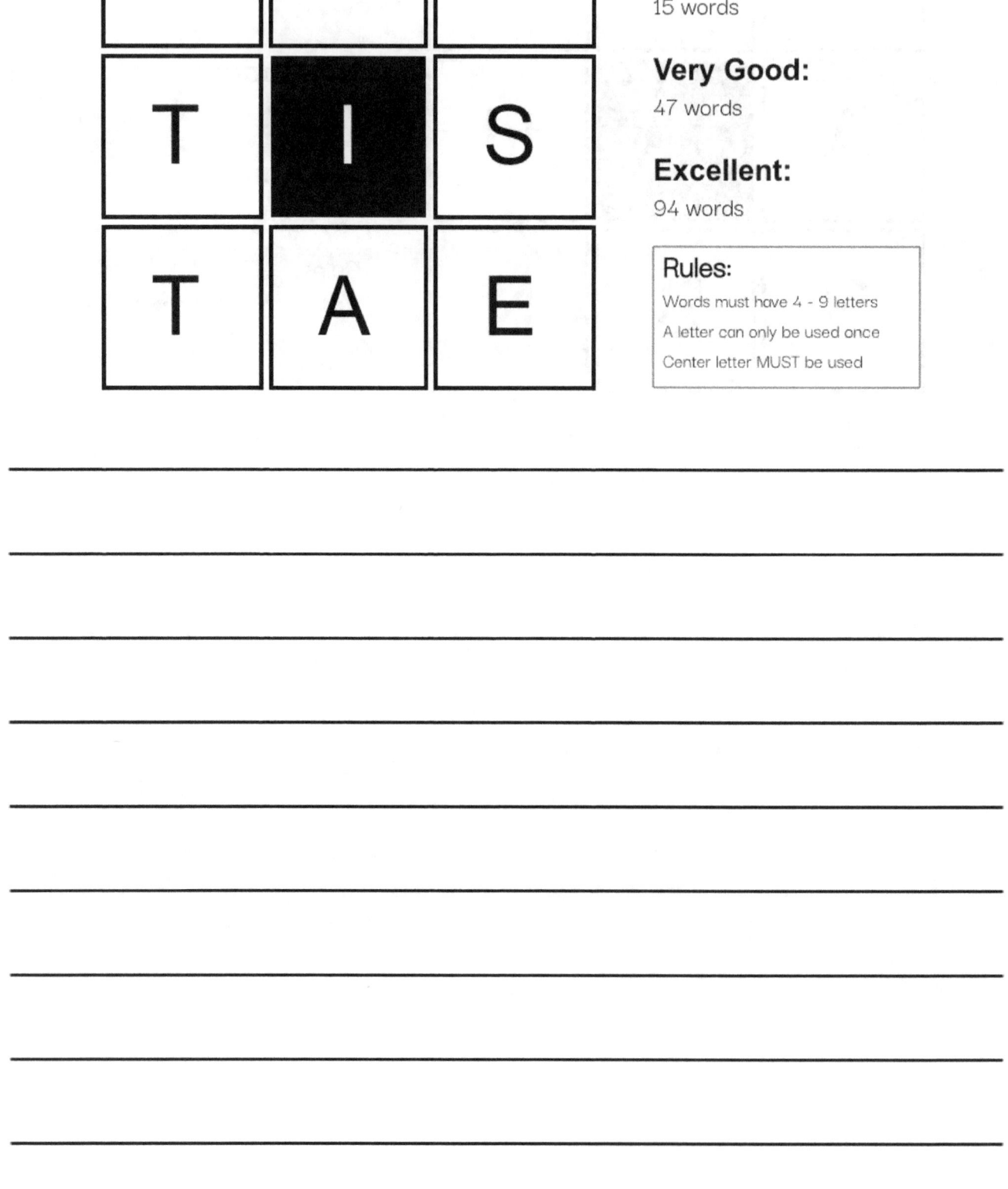

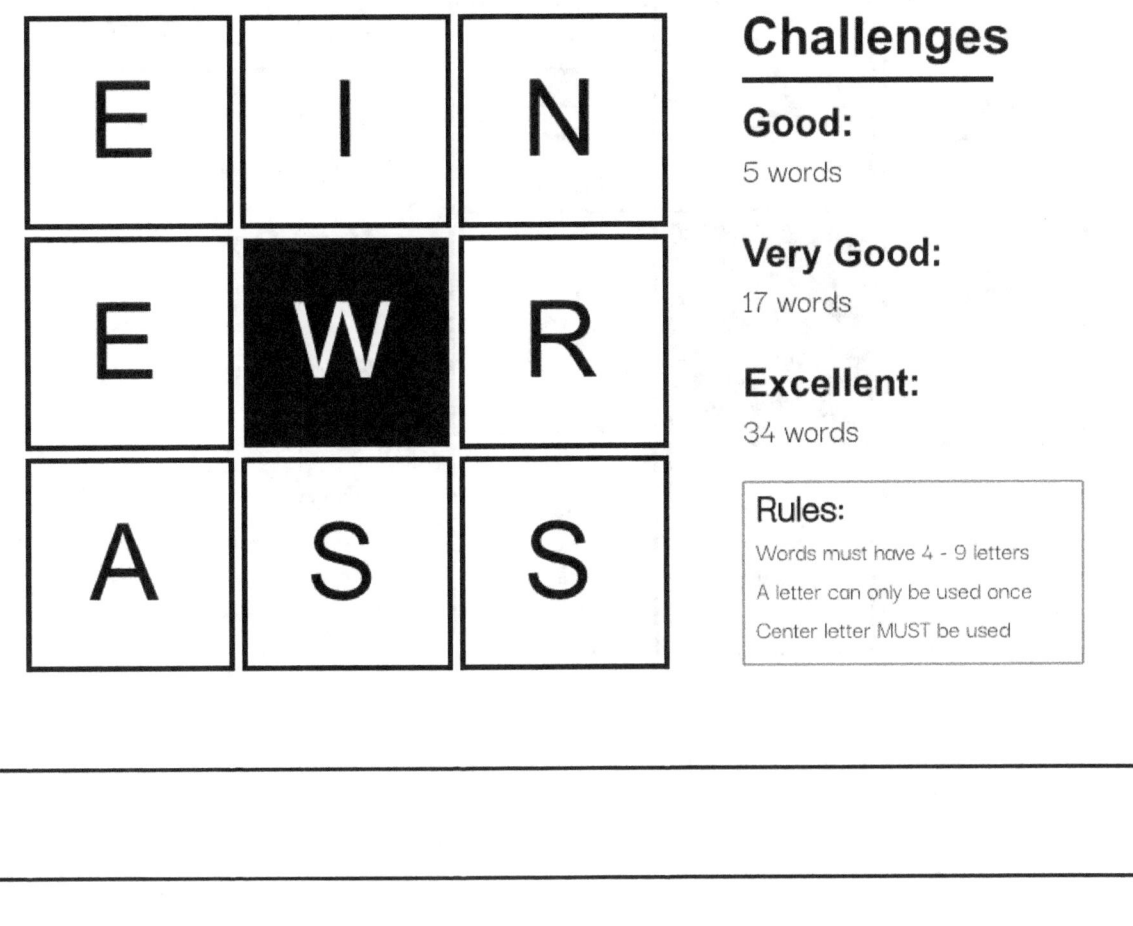

Challenges

Good:
5 words

Very Good:
17 words

Excellent:
34 words

Rules:
Words must have 4 - 9 letters
A letter can only be used once
Center letter MUST be used

Challenges

Good:
1 words

Very Good:
5 words

Excellent:
10 words

Rules:
Words must have 4 - 9 letters
A letter can only be used once
Center letter MUST be used

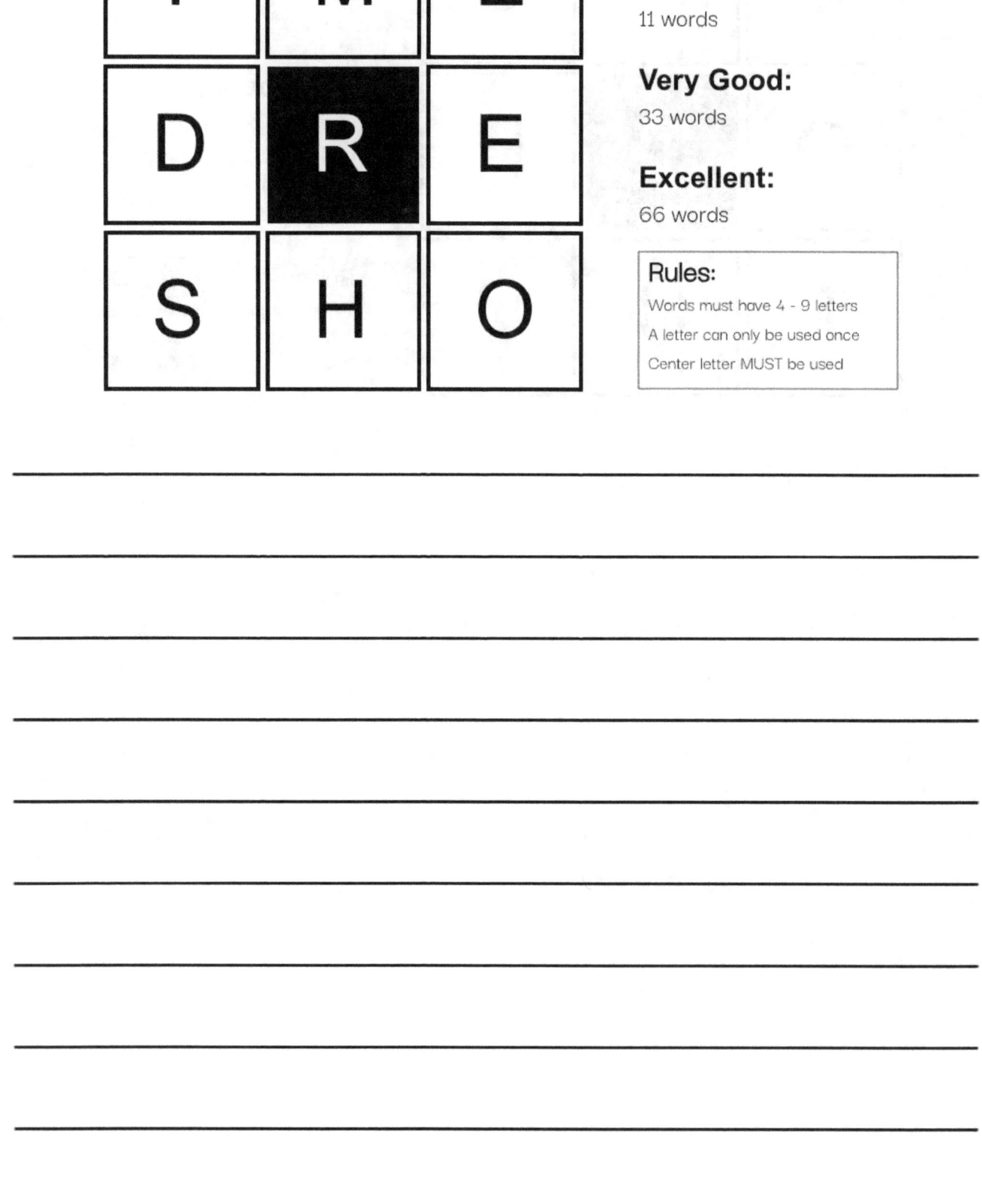

Challenges

Good:
9 words

Very Good:
27 words

Excellent:
54 words

Rules:
Words must have 4 - 9 letters
A letter can only be used once
Center letter MUST be used

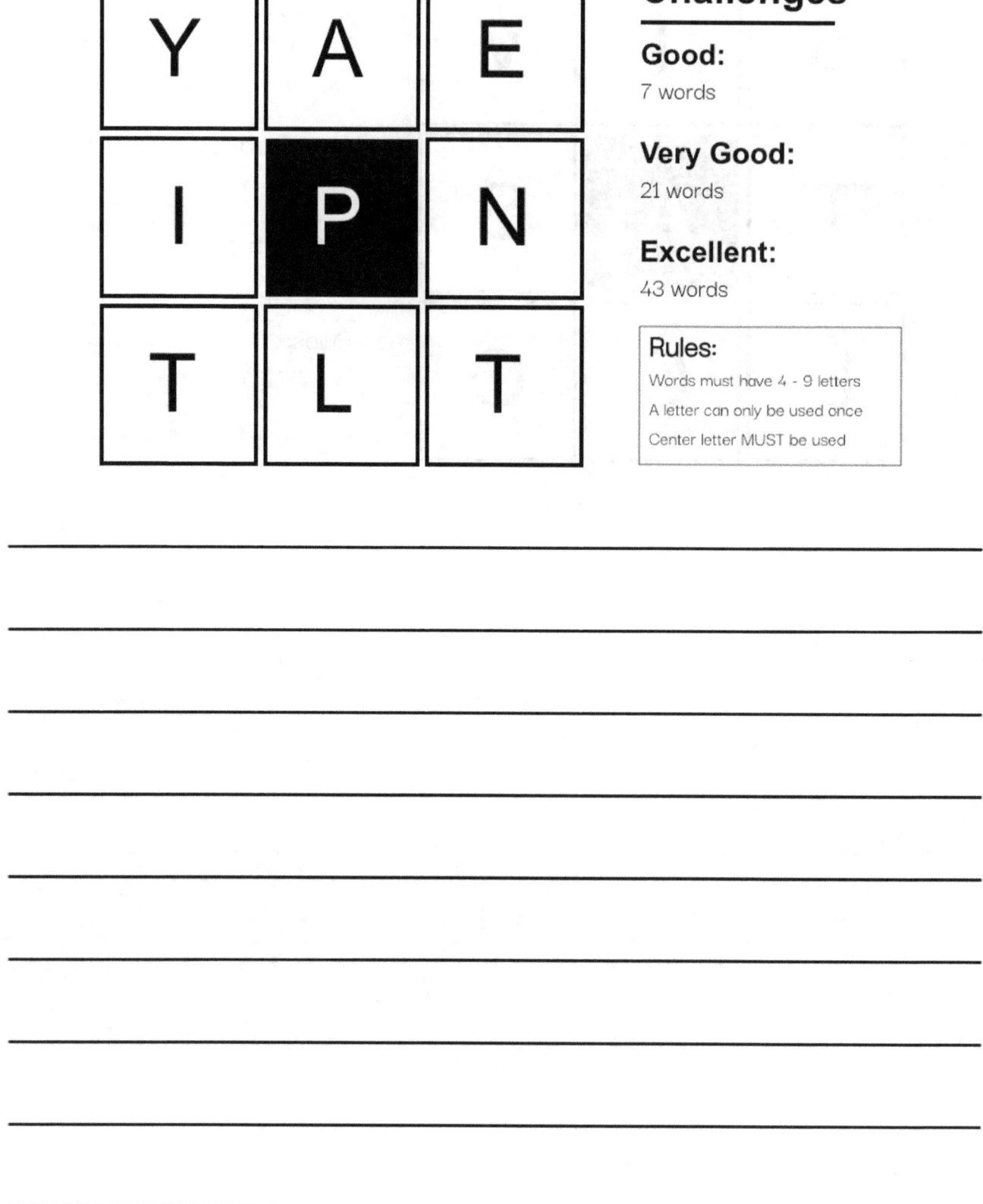

Challenges

Good:
8 words

Very Good:
26 words

Excellent:
52 words

Rules:
Words must have 4 - 9 letters
A letter can only be used once
Center letter MUST be used

13

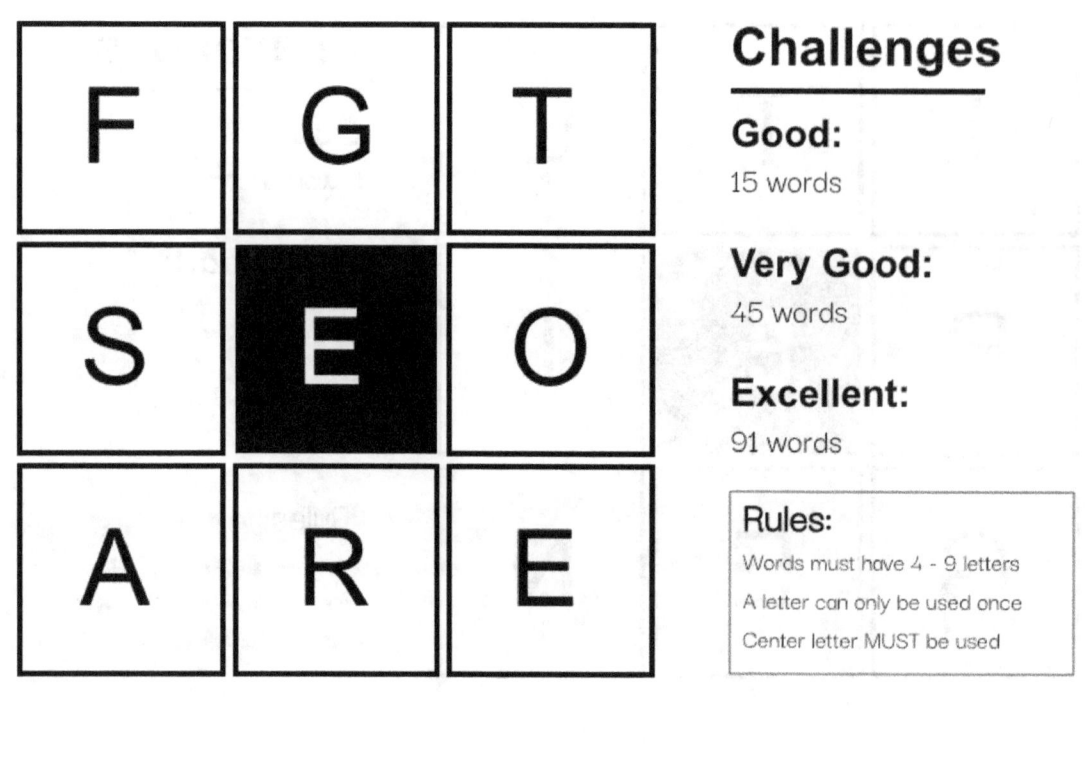

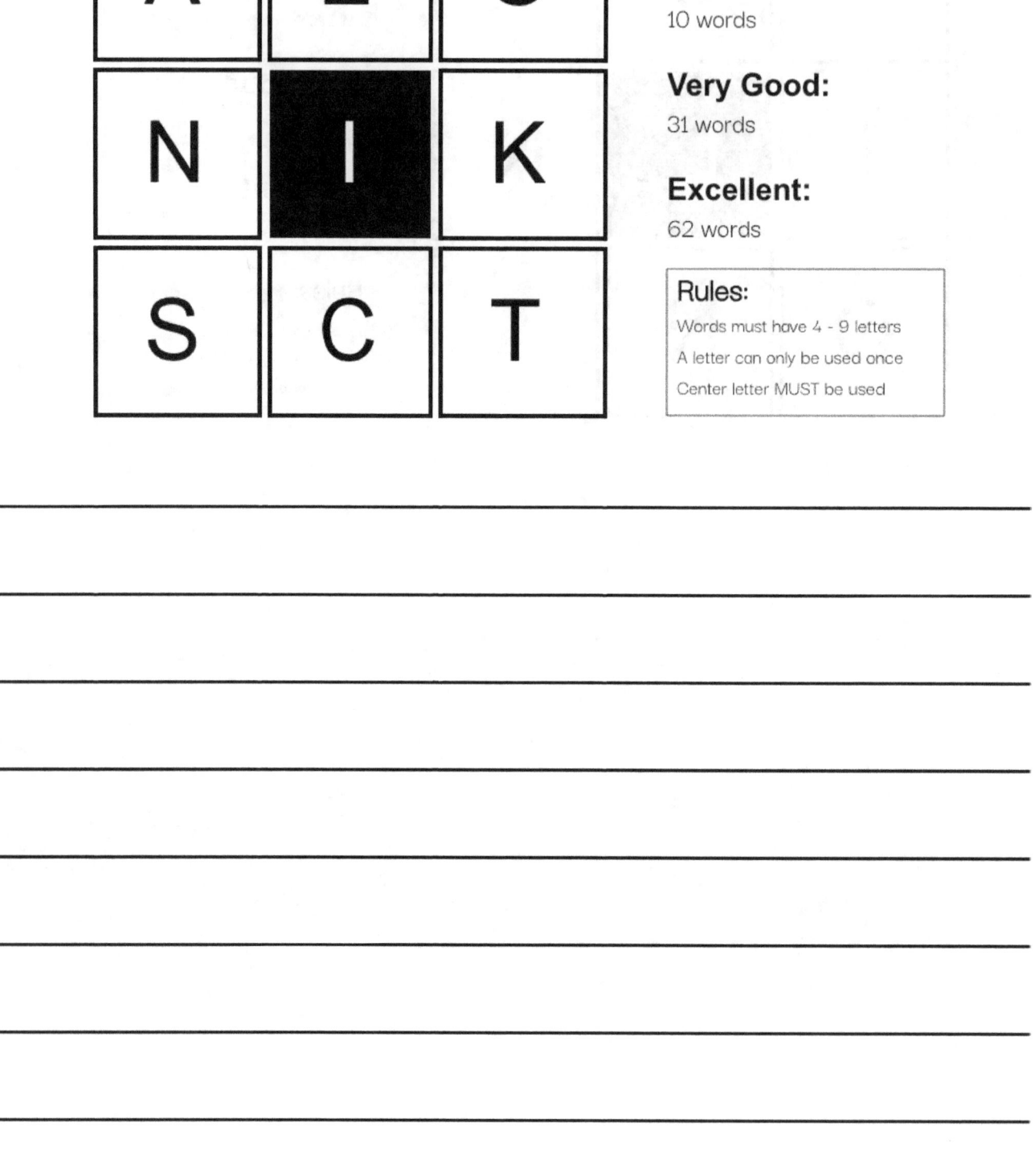

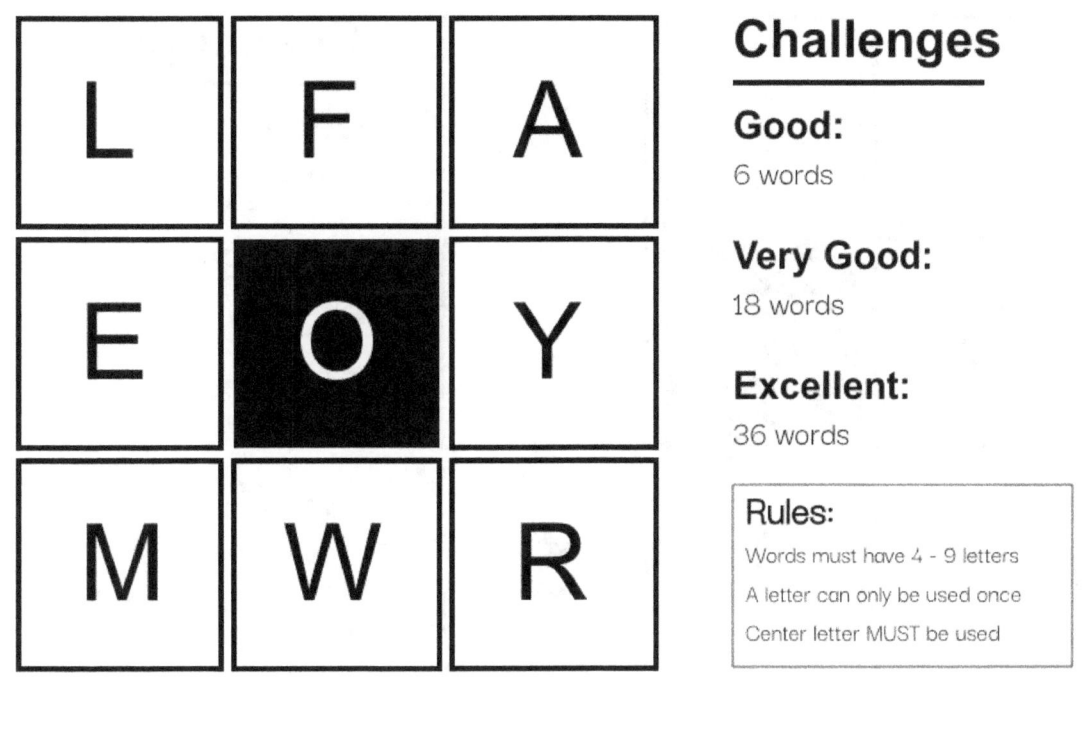

Challenges

Good:
6 words

Very Good:
18 words

Excellent:
36 words

Rules:
Words must have 4 - 9 letters
A letter can only be used once
Center letter MUST be used

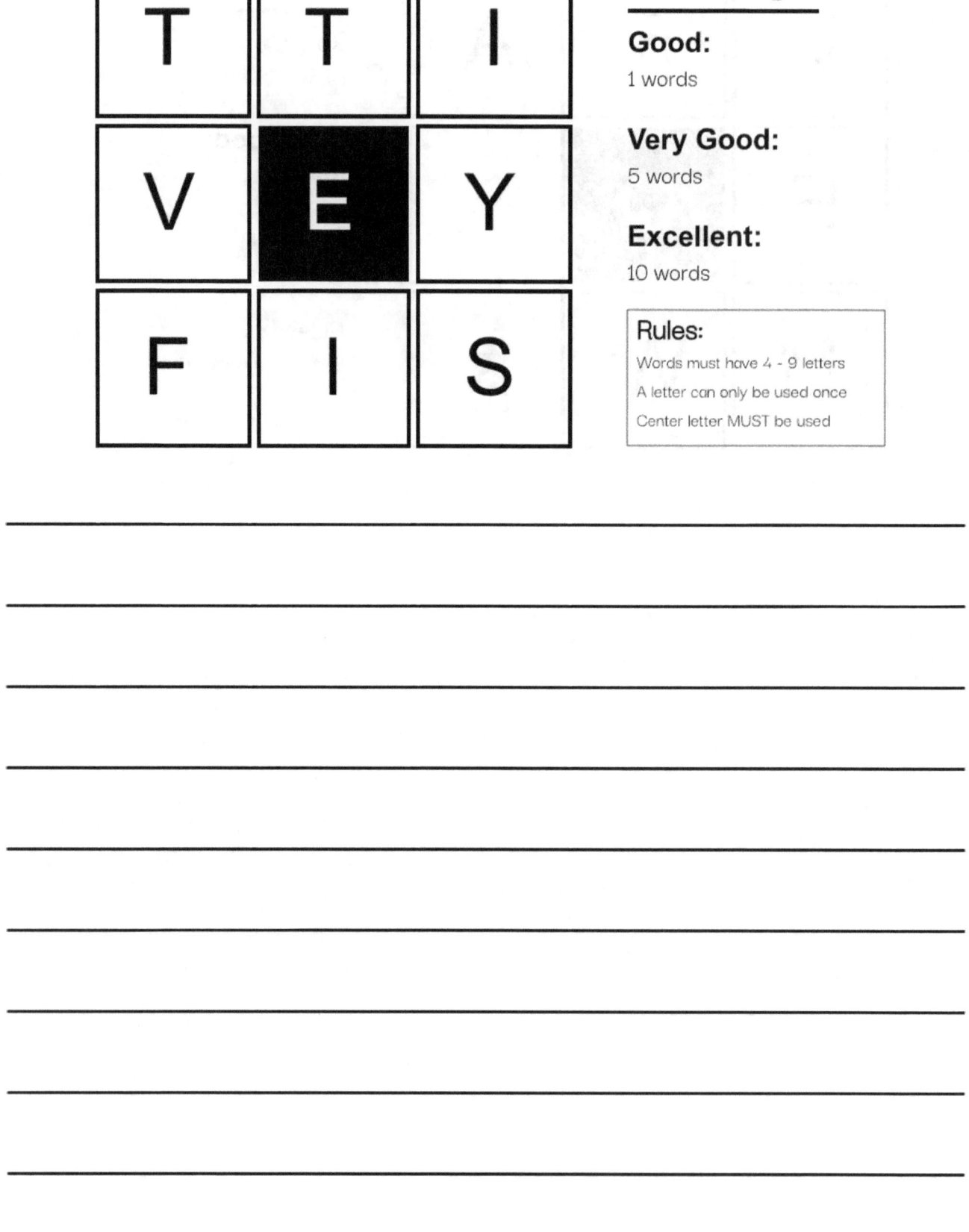

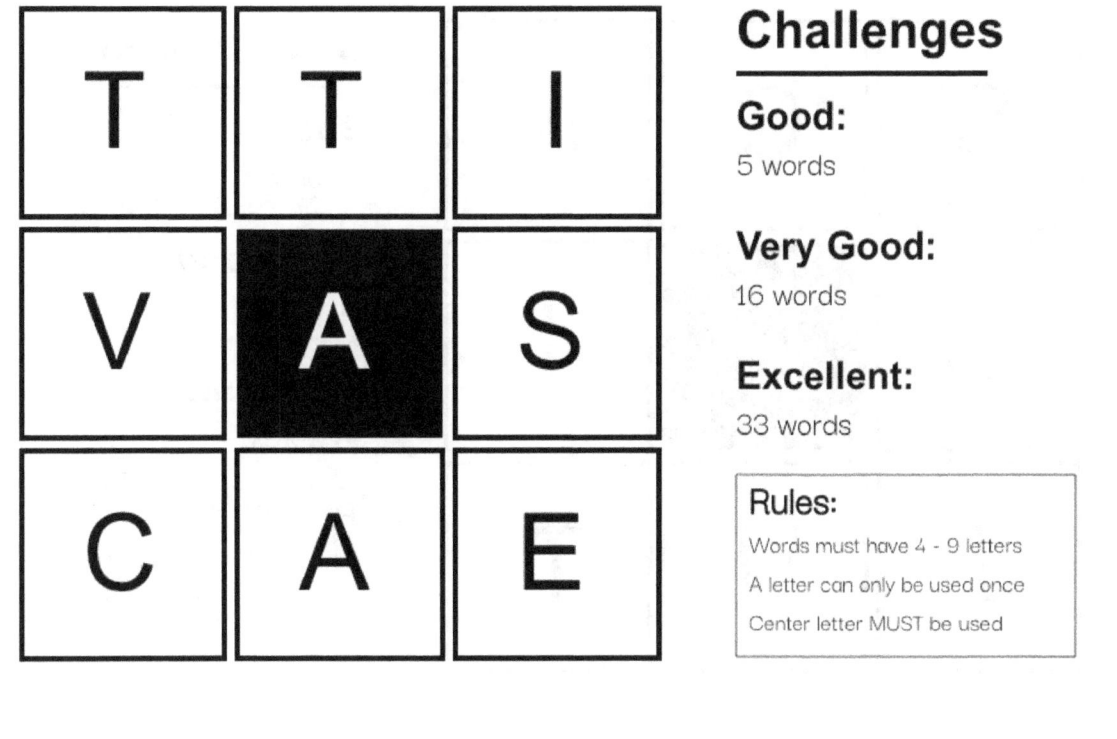

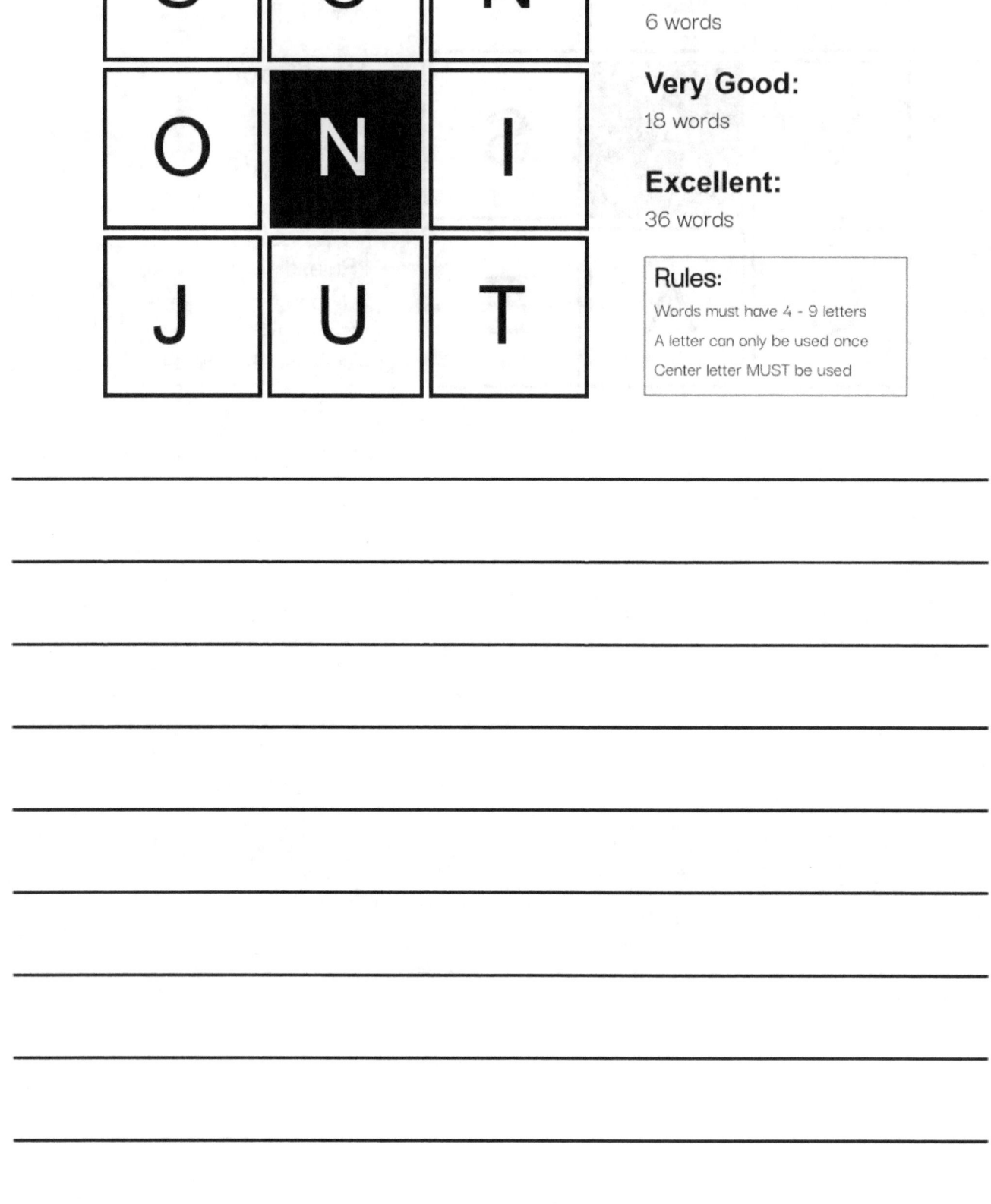

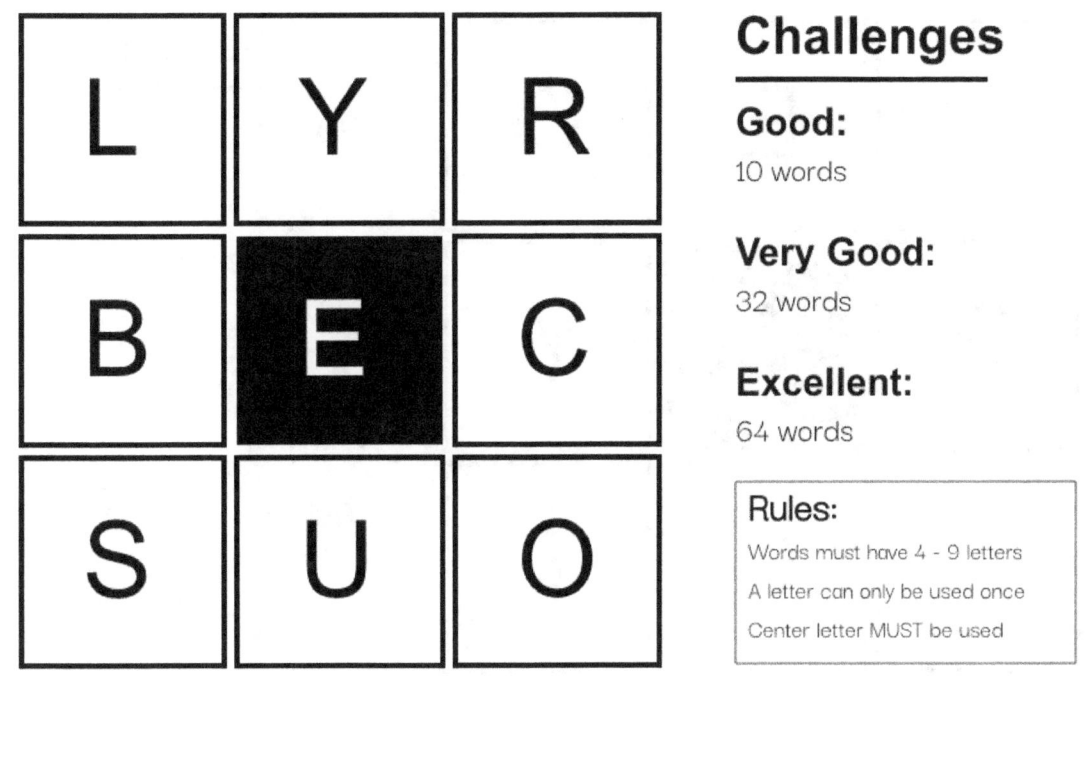

Challenges

Good:
10 words

Very Good:
32 words

Excellent:
64 words

Rules:
Words must have 4 - 9 letters
A letter can only be used once
Center letter MUST be used

Challenges

Good:
8 words

Very Good:
24 words

Excellent:
49 words

Rules:
Words must have 4 - 9 letters
A letter can only be used once
Center letter MUST be used

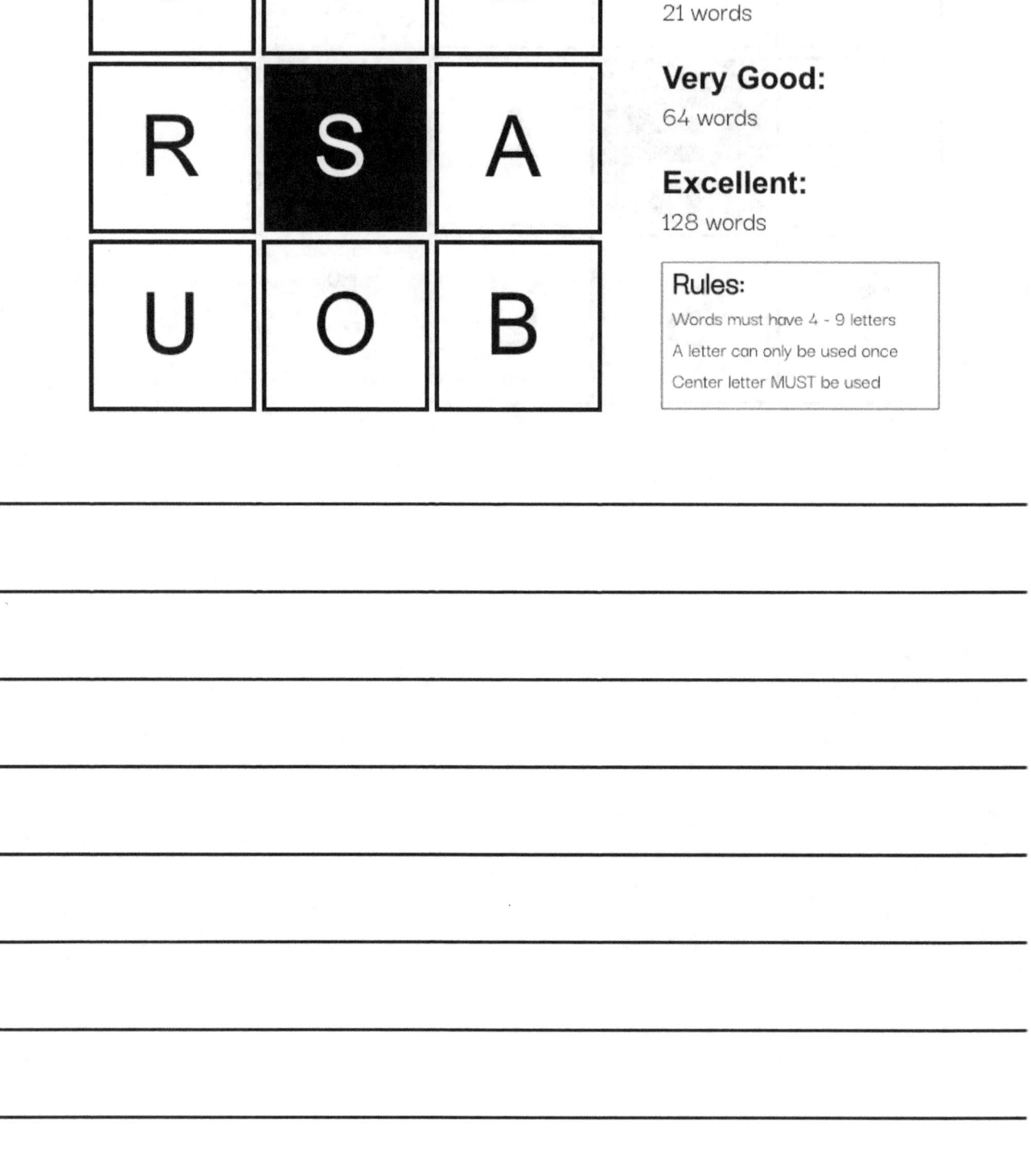

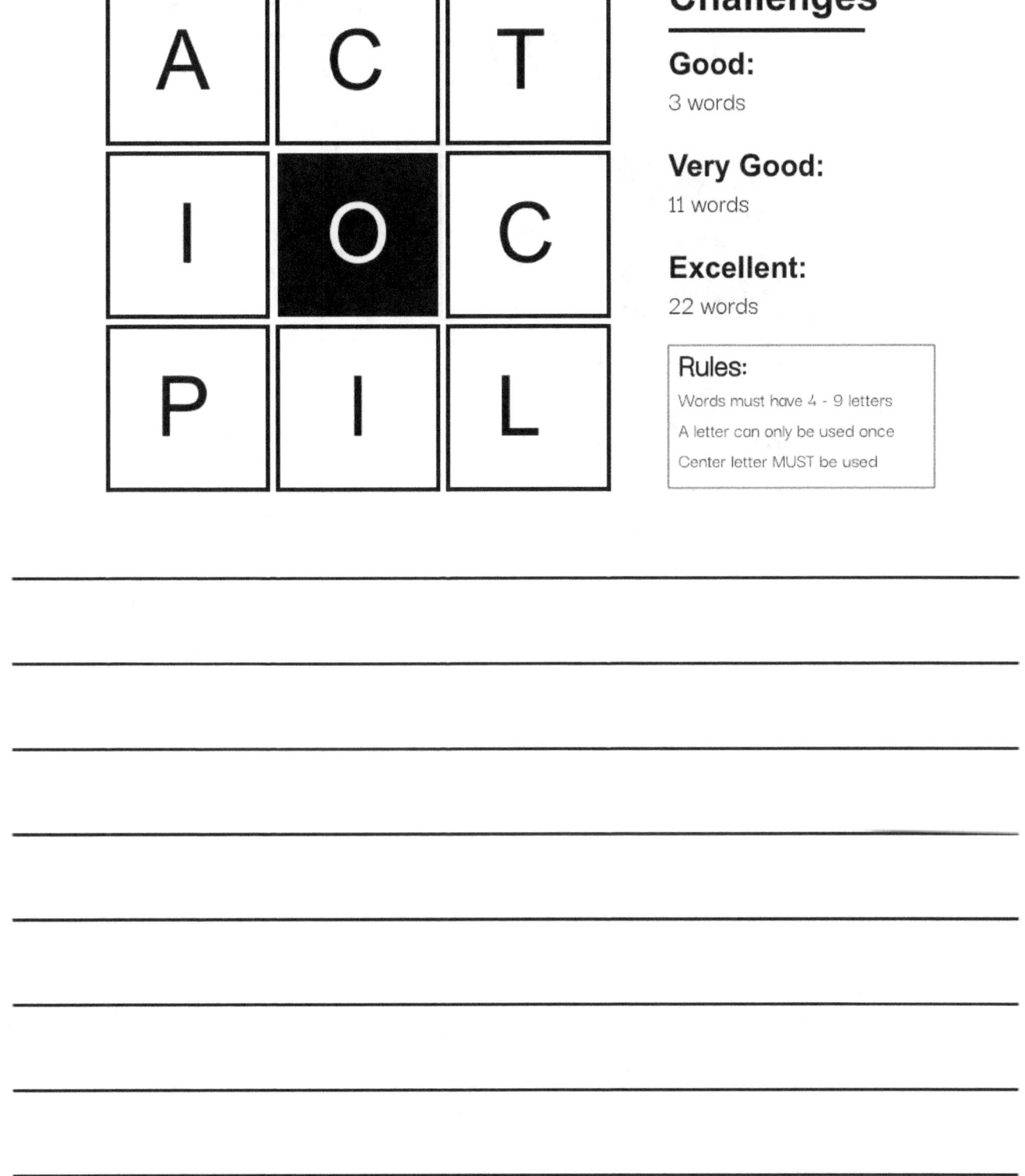

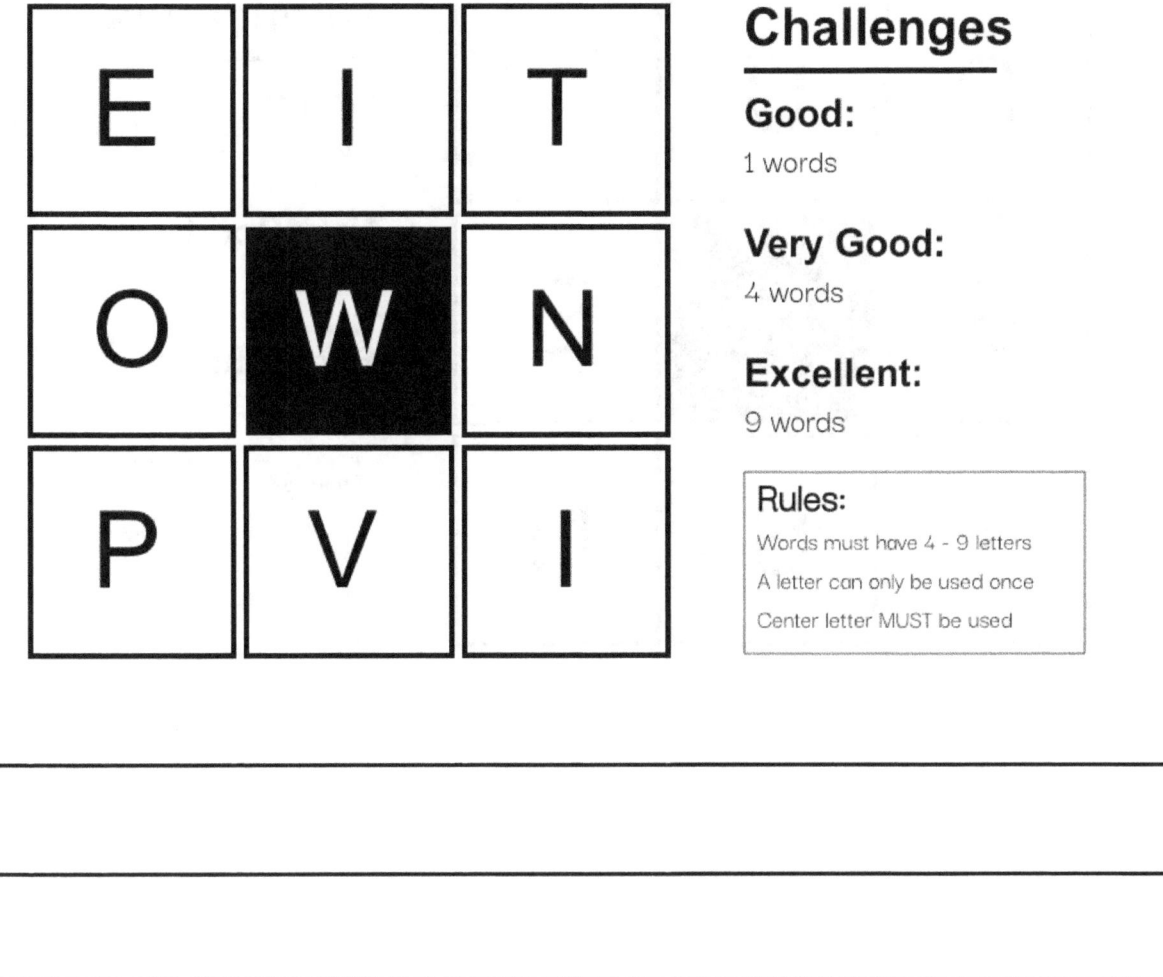

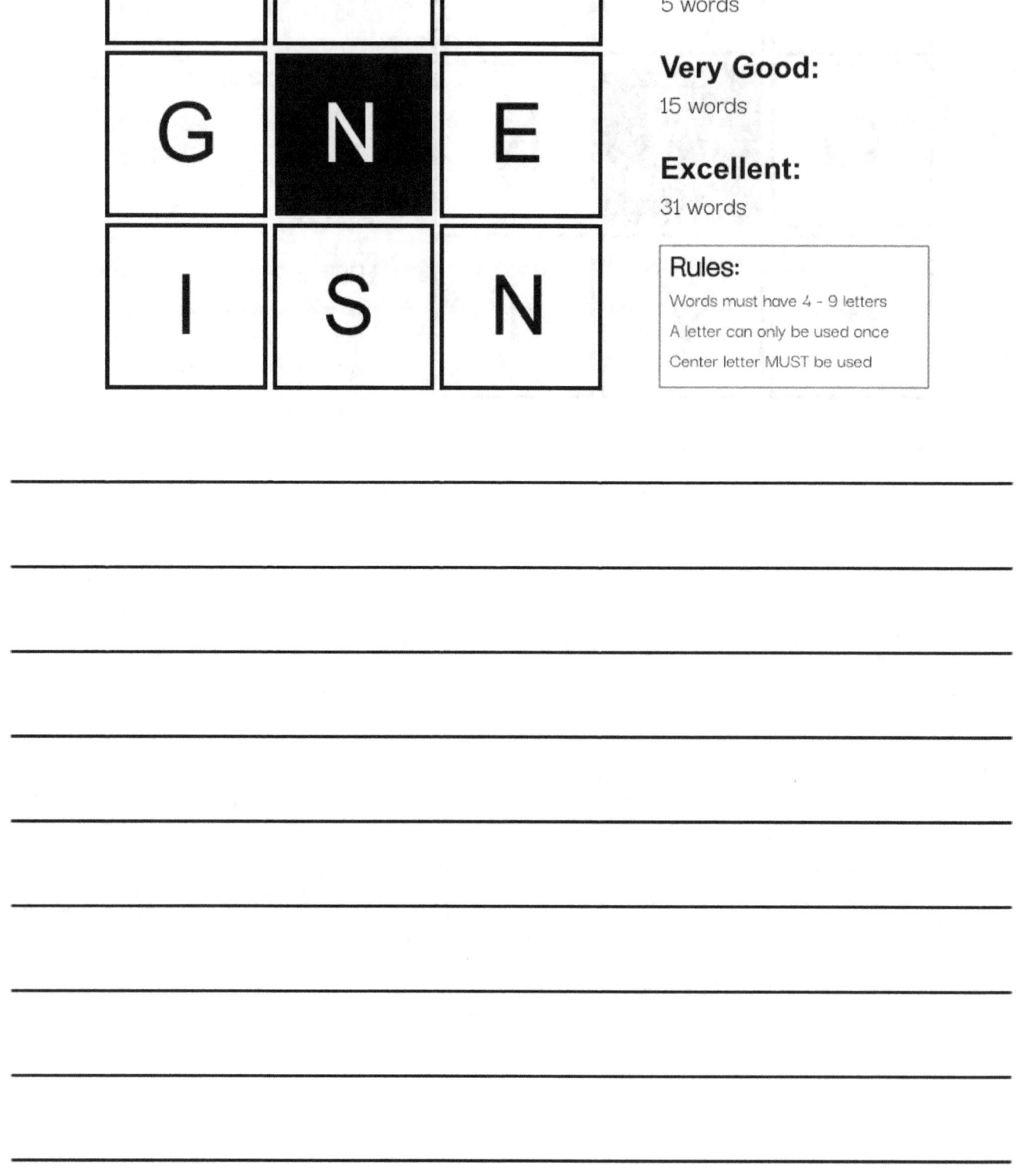

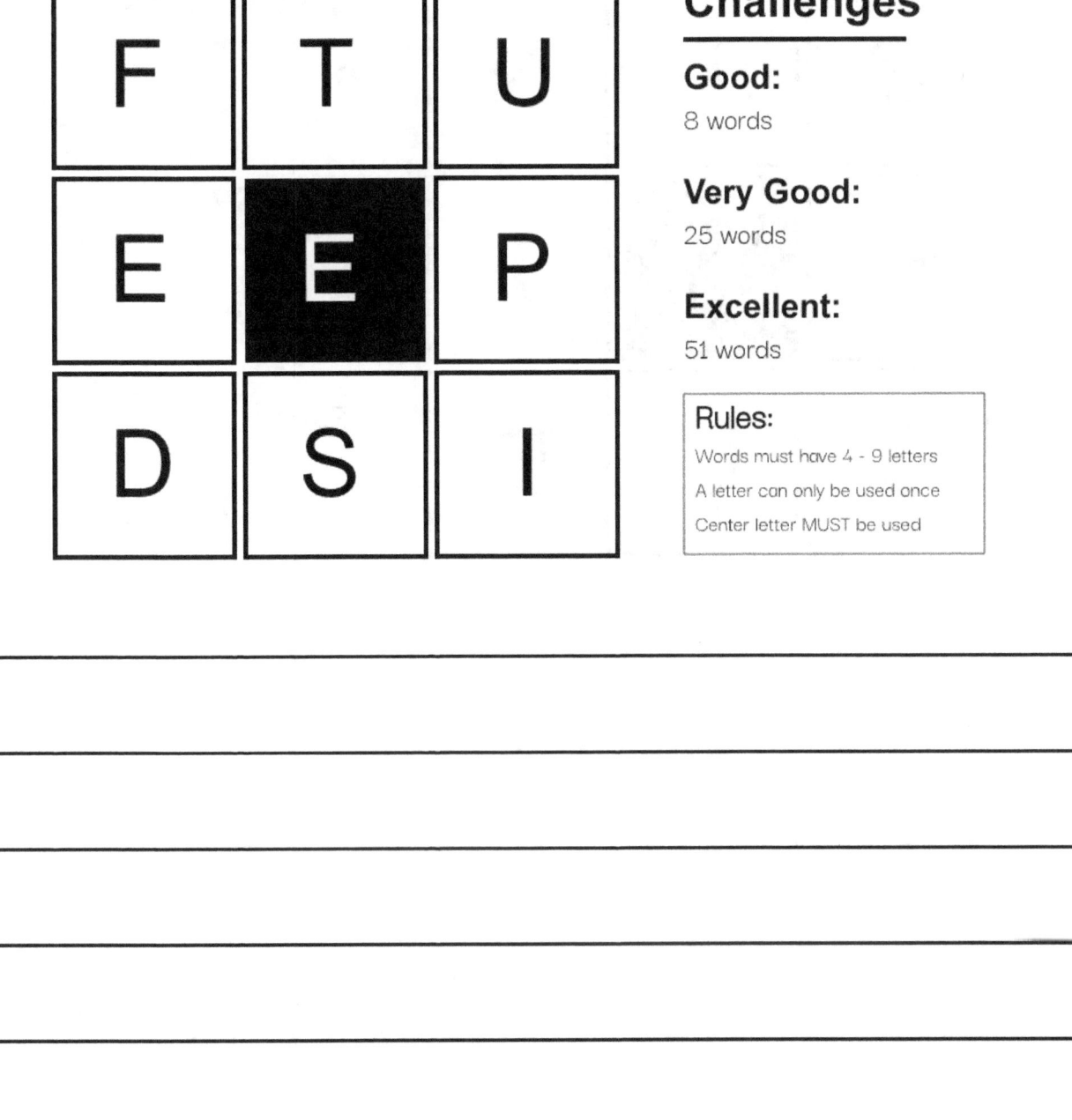

Challenges

Good:
8 words

Very Good:
25 words

Excellent:
51 words

Rules:
Words must have 4 - 9 letters
A letter can only be used once
Center letter MUST be used

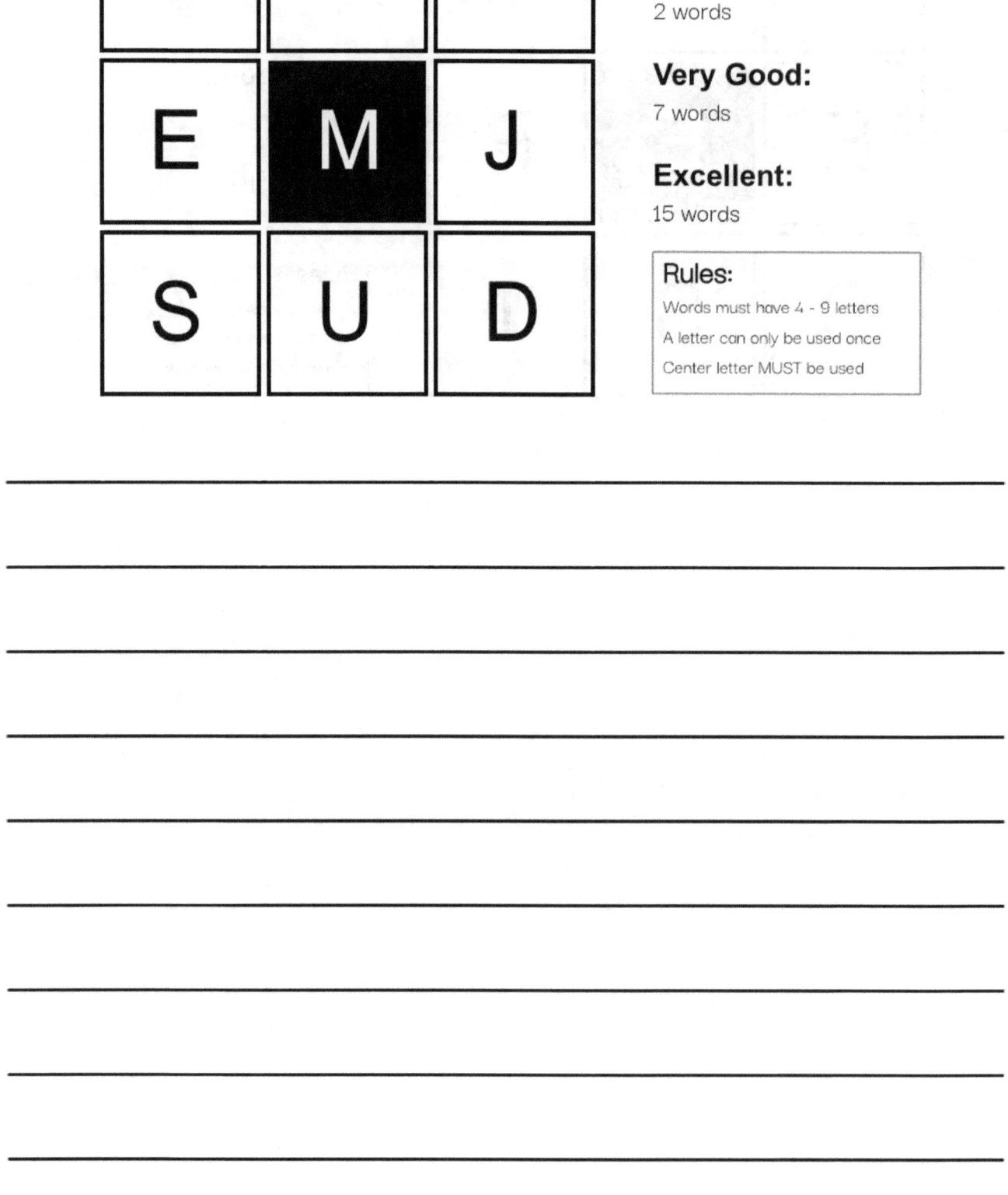

Challenges

Good:
2 words

Very Good:
7 words

Excellent:
15 words

Rules:
Words must have 4 - 9 letters
A letter can only be used once
Center letter MUST be used

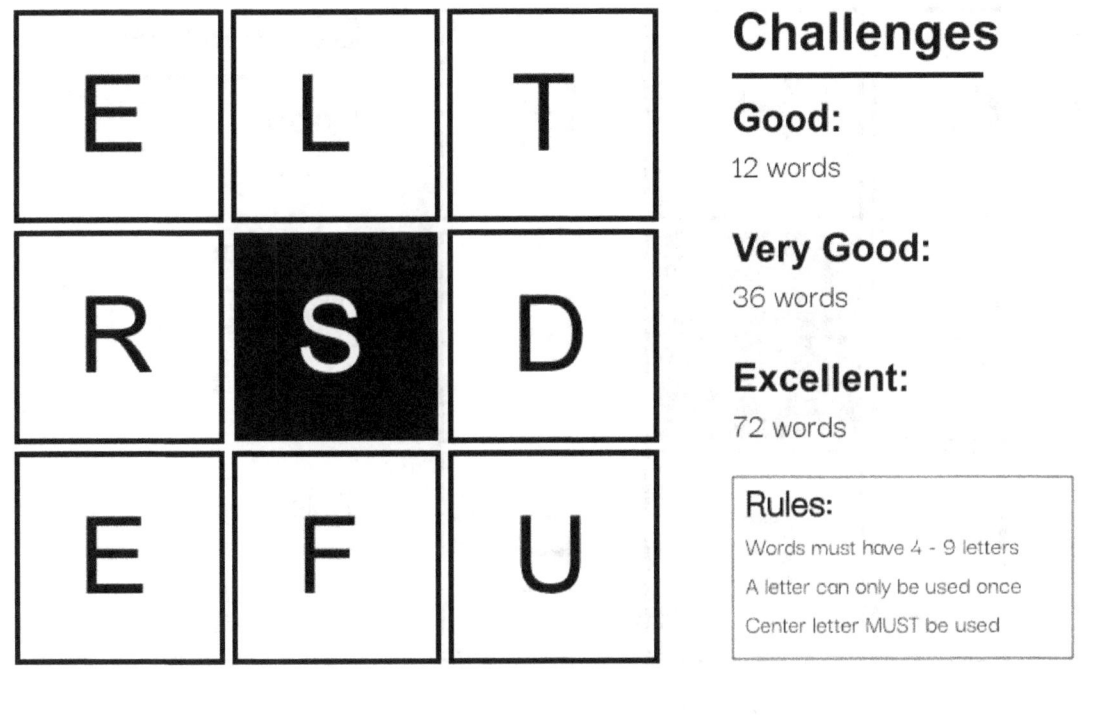

Challenges

Good:
12 words

Very Good:
36 words

Excellent:
72 words

Rules:
Words must have 4 - 9 letters
A letter can only be used once
Center letter MUST be used

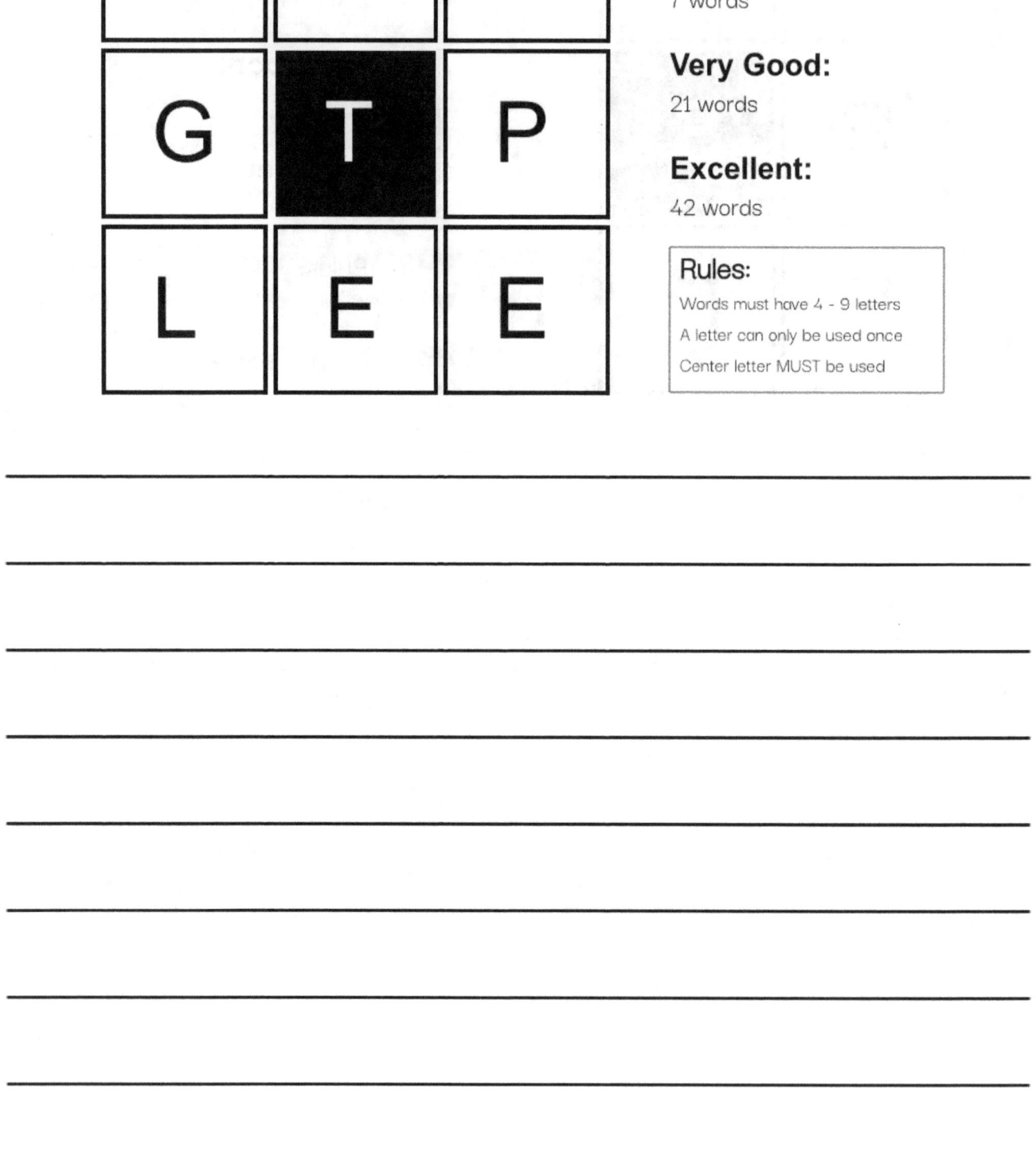

Challenges

Good:
7 words

Very Good:
21 words

Excellent:
42 words

Rules:
Words must have 4 - 9 letters
A letter can only be used once
Center letter MUST be used

Challenges

Good:
3 words

Very Good:
11 words

Excellent:
22 words

Rules:
Words must have 4 - 9 letters
A letter can only be used once
Center letter MUST be used

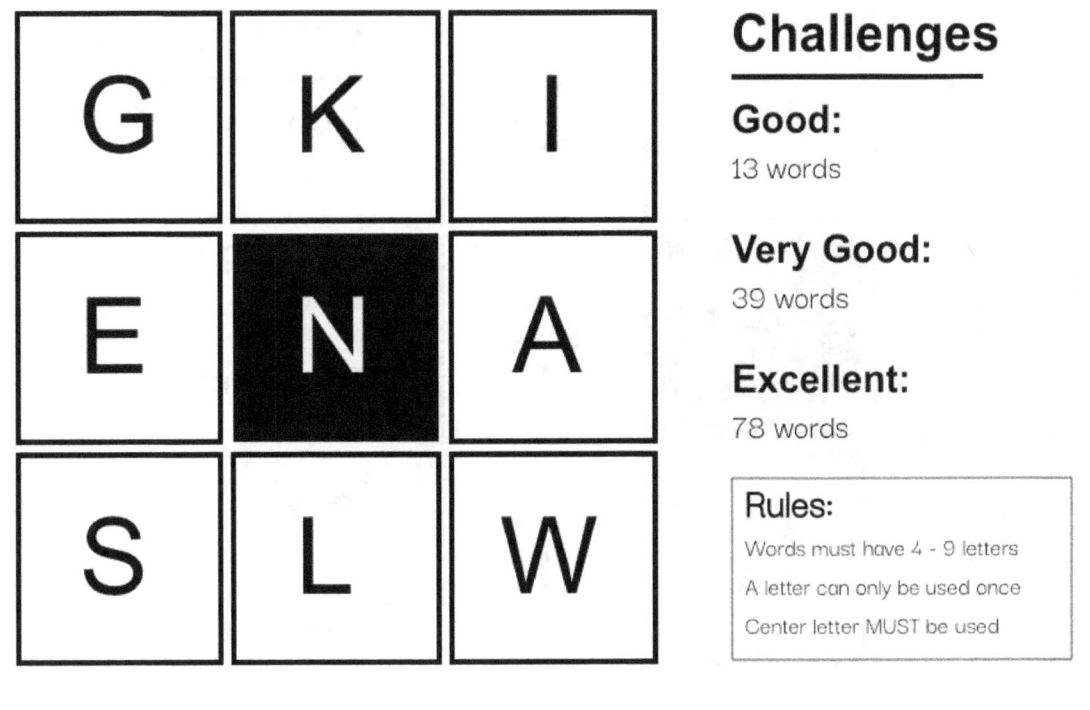

Challenges

Good:
13 words

Very Good:
39 words

Excellent:
78 words

Rules:
Words must have 4 - 9 letters
A letter can only be used once
Center letter MUST be used

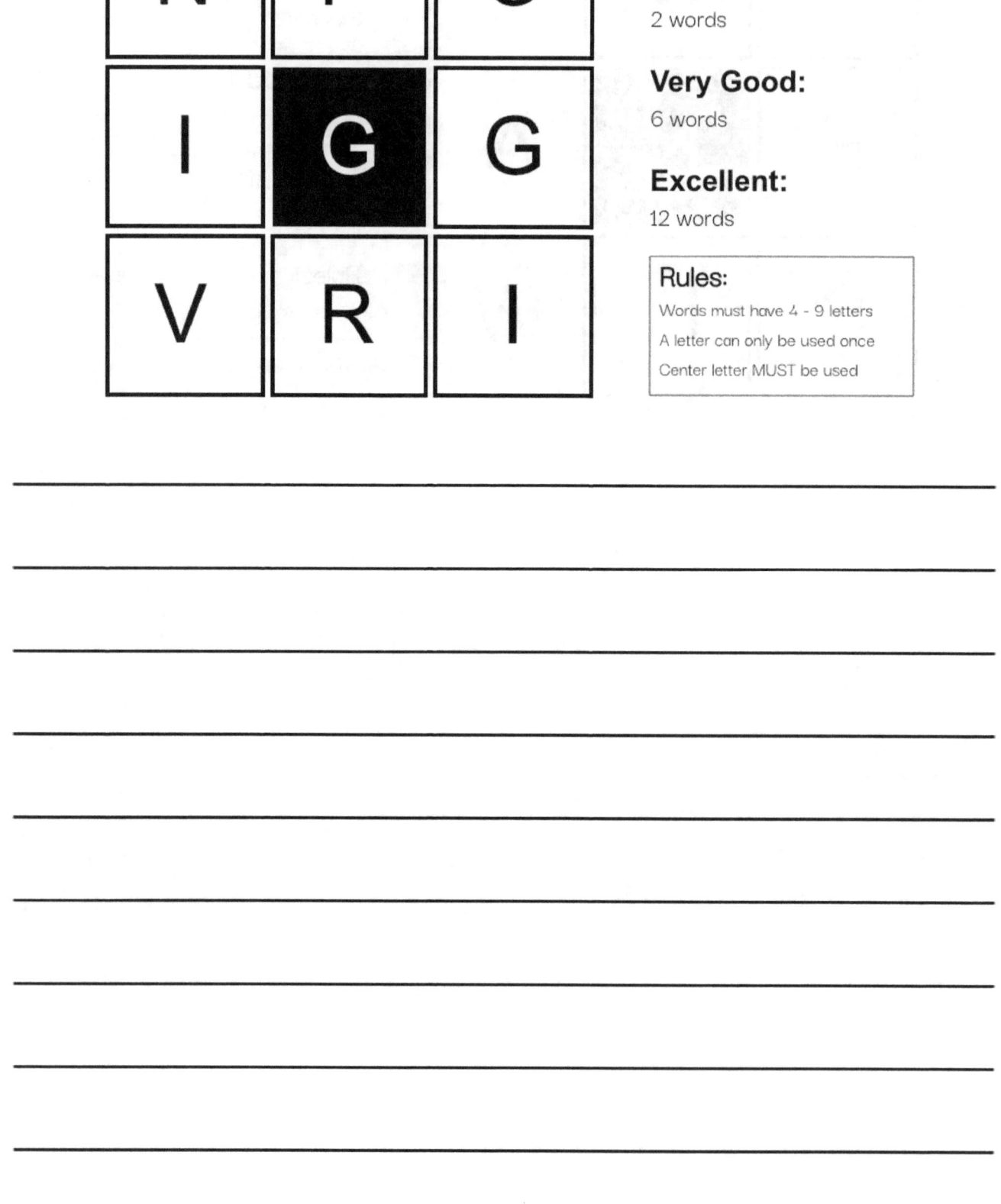

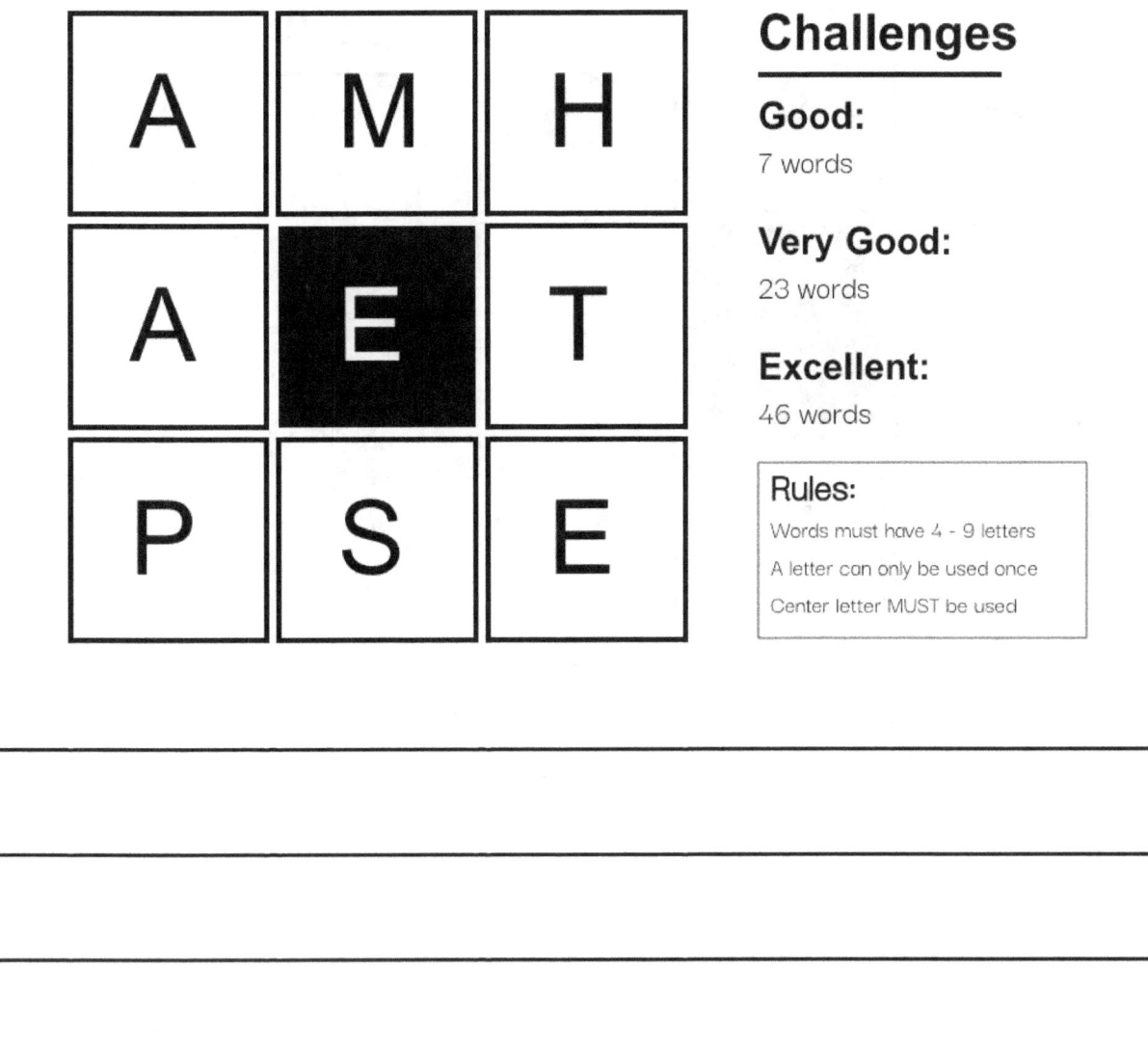

Challenges

Good:
7 words

Very Good:
23 words

Excellent:
46 words

Rules:
Words must have 4 - 9 letters
A letter can only be used once
Center letter MUST be used

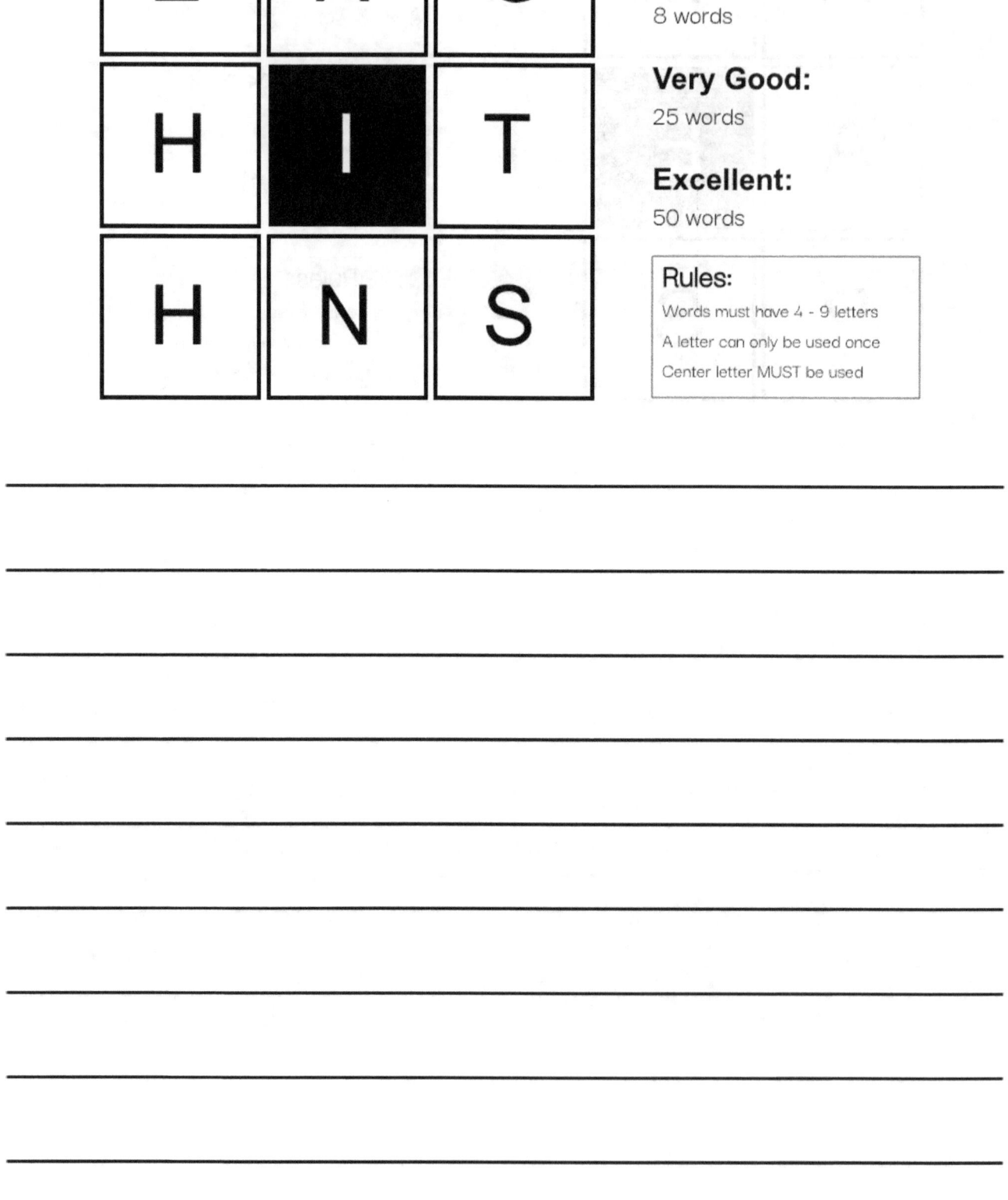

38

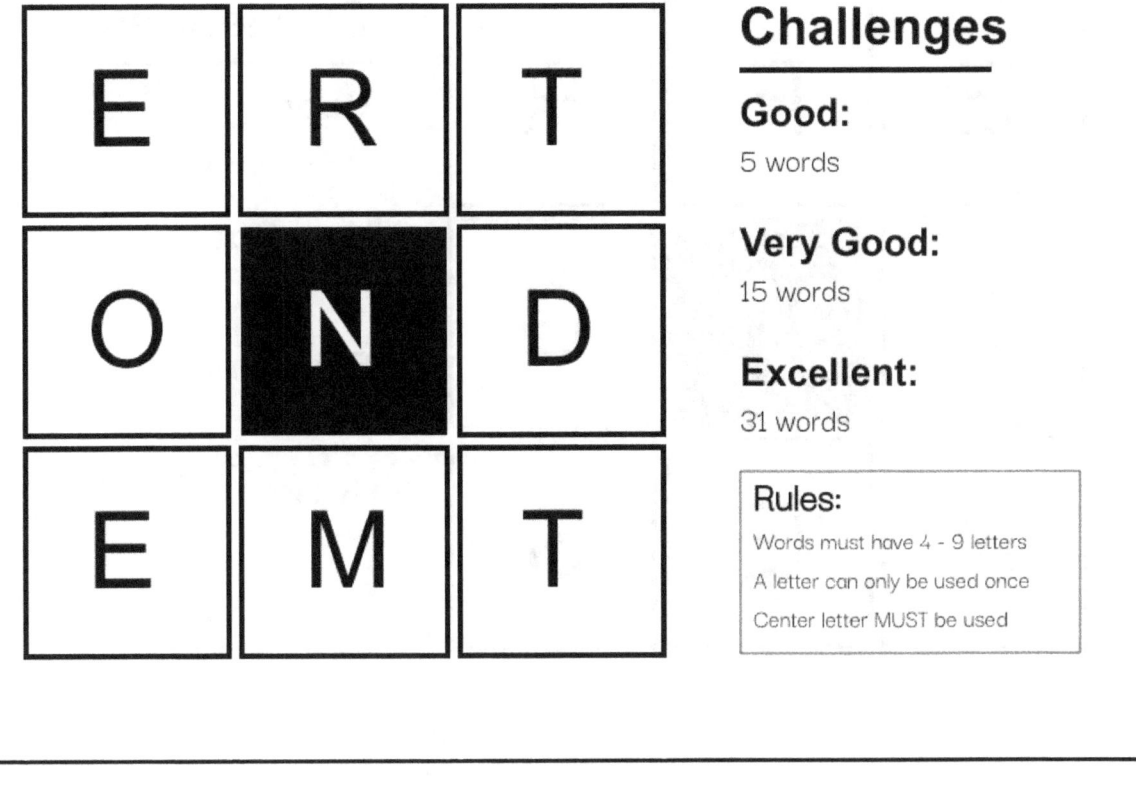

Challenges

Good:
5 words

Very Good:
15 words

Excellent:
31 words

Rules:
Words must have 4 - 9 letters
A letter can only be used once
Center letter MUST be used

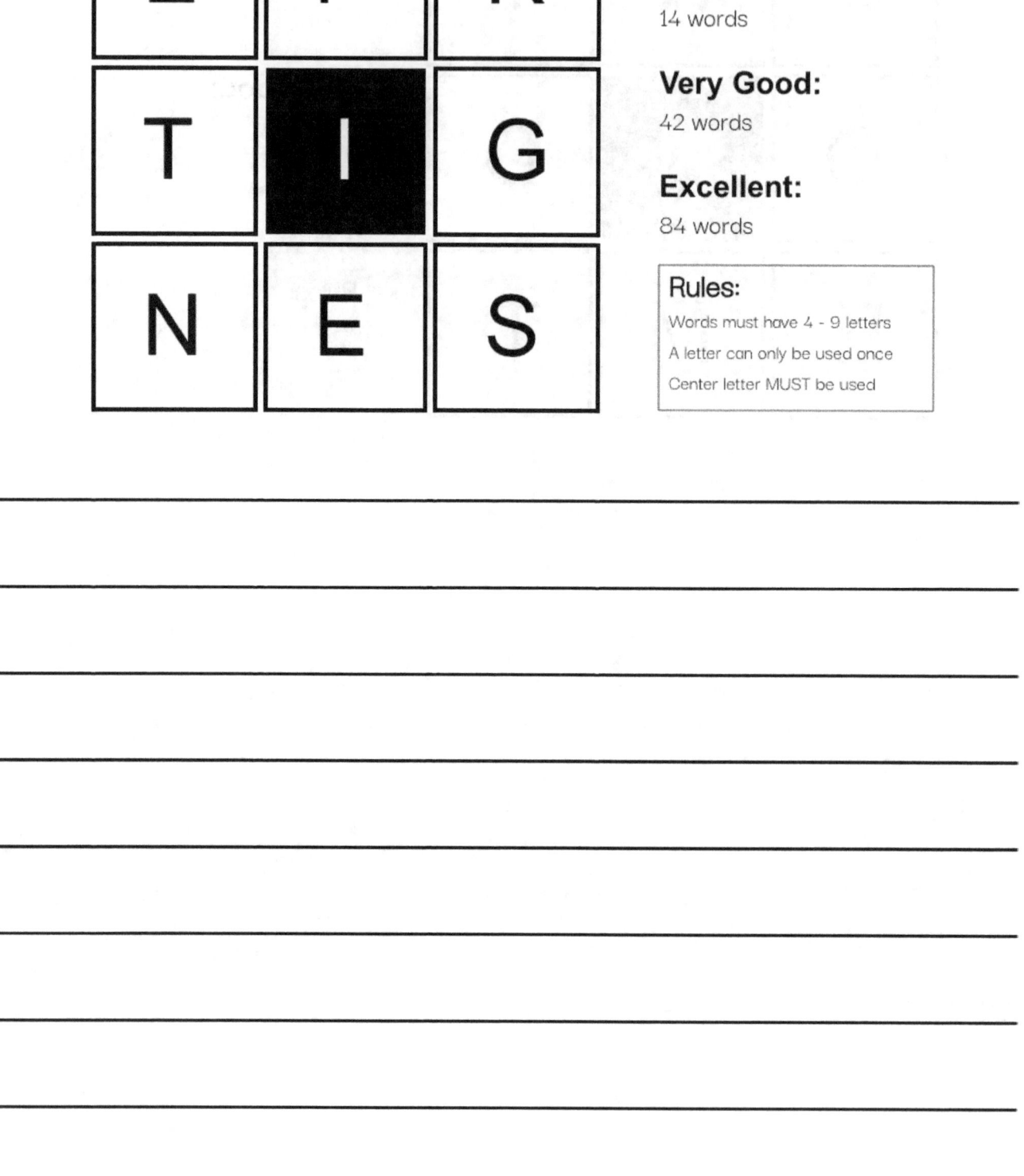

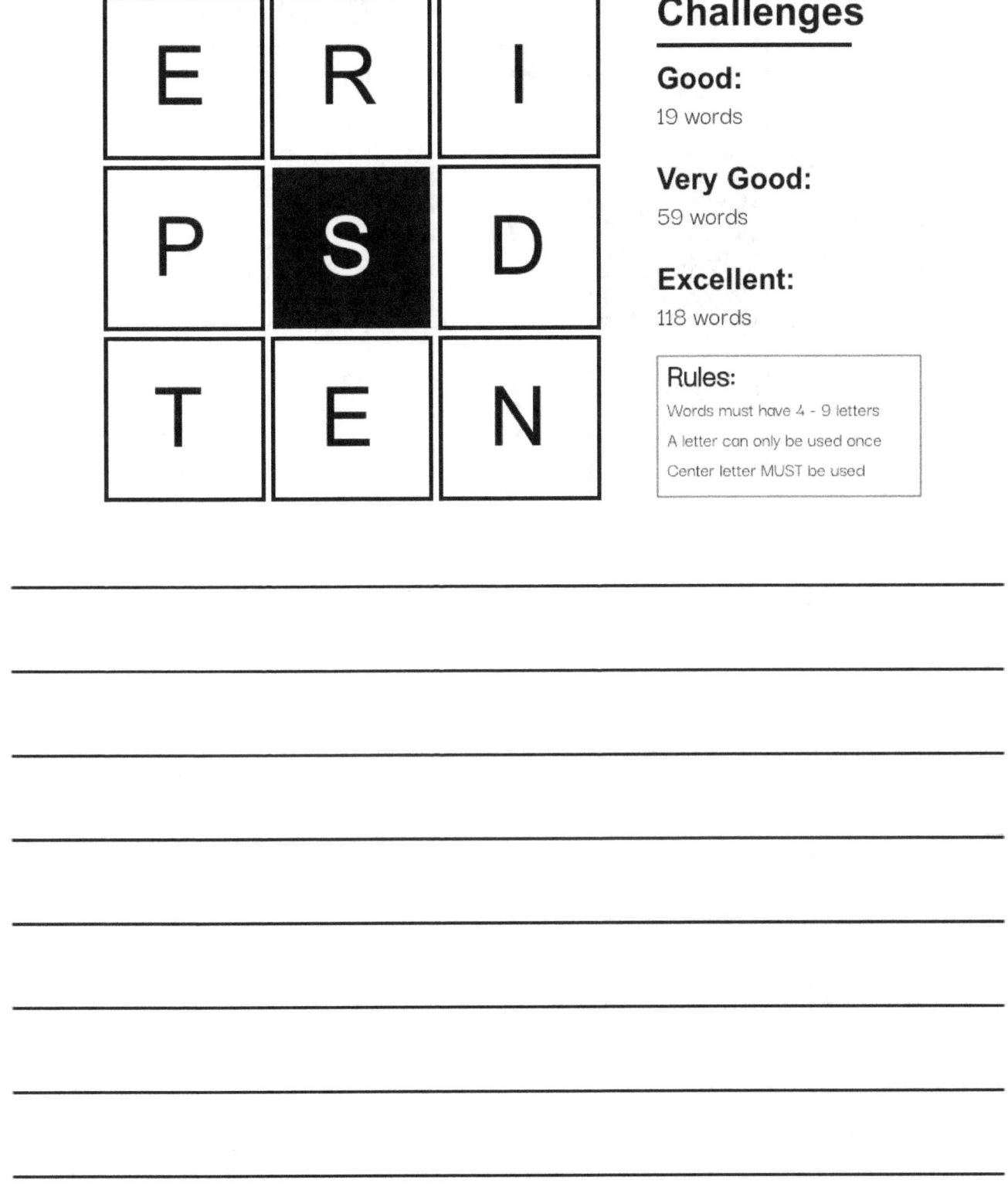

Challenges

Good:
19 words

Very Good:
59 words

Excellent:
118 words

Rules:
Words must have 4 - 9 letters
A letter can only be used once
Center letter MUST be used

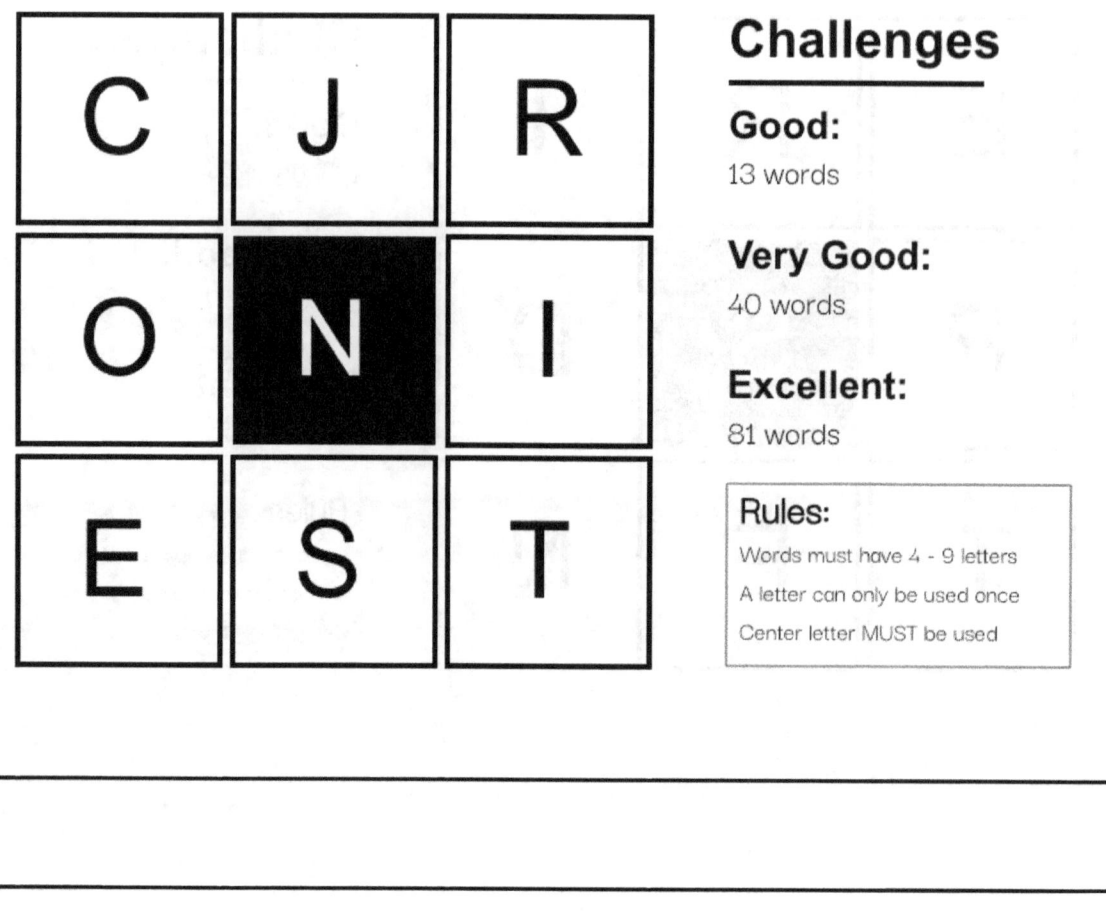

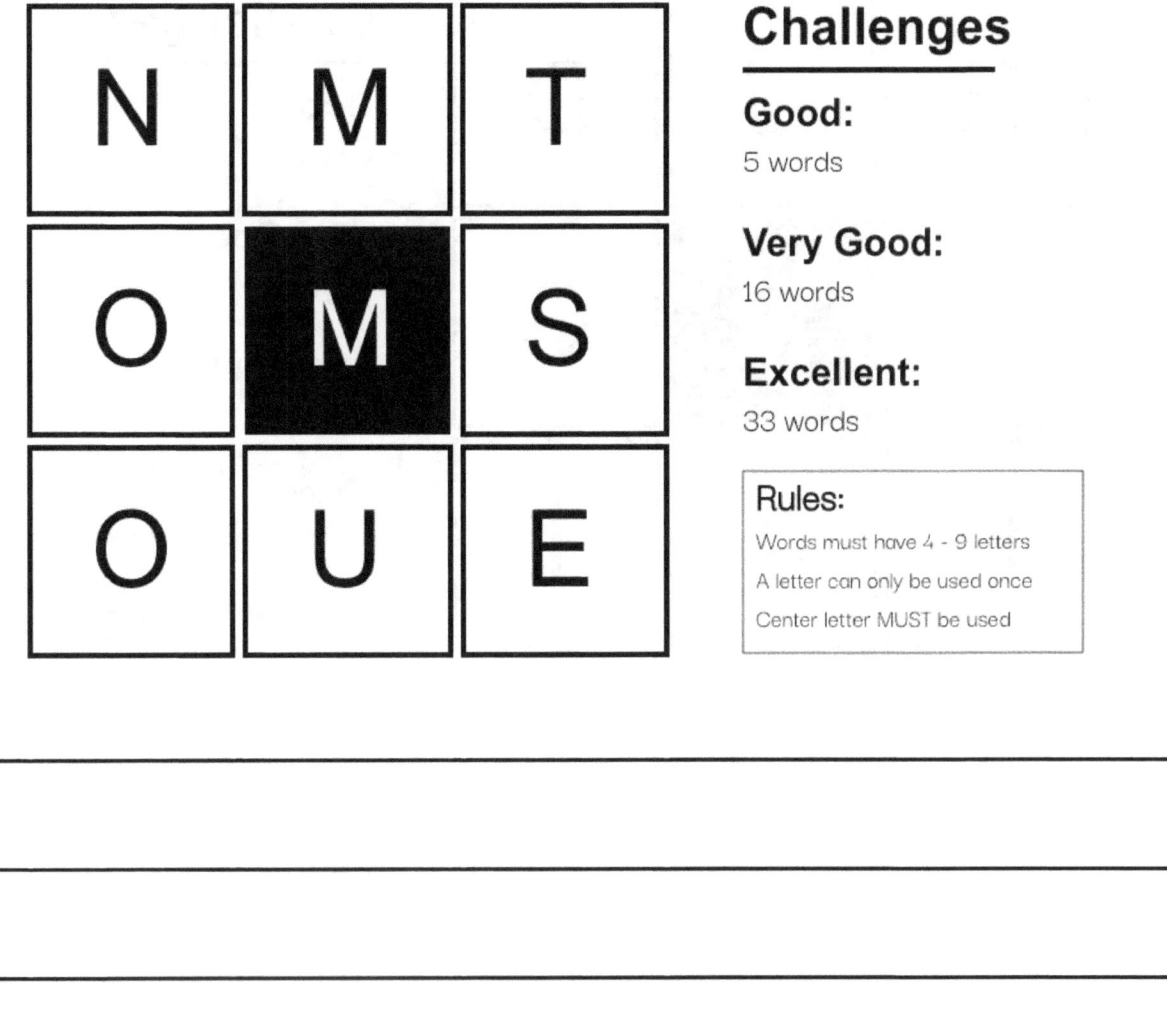

Challenges

Good:
4 words

Very Good:
13 words

Excellent:
26 words

Rules:
Words must have 4 - 9 letters
A letter can only be used once
Center letter MUST be used

44

Letter grid:
N	G	T
S	**E**	L
N	I	I

Challenges

Good:
8 words

Very Good:
25 words

Excellent:
50 words

Rules:
Words must have 4 - 9 letters
A letter can only be used once
Center letter MUST be used

45

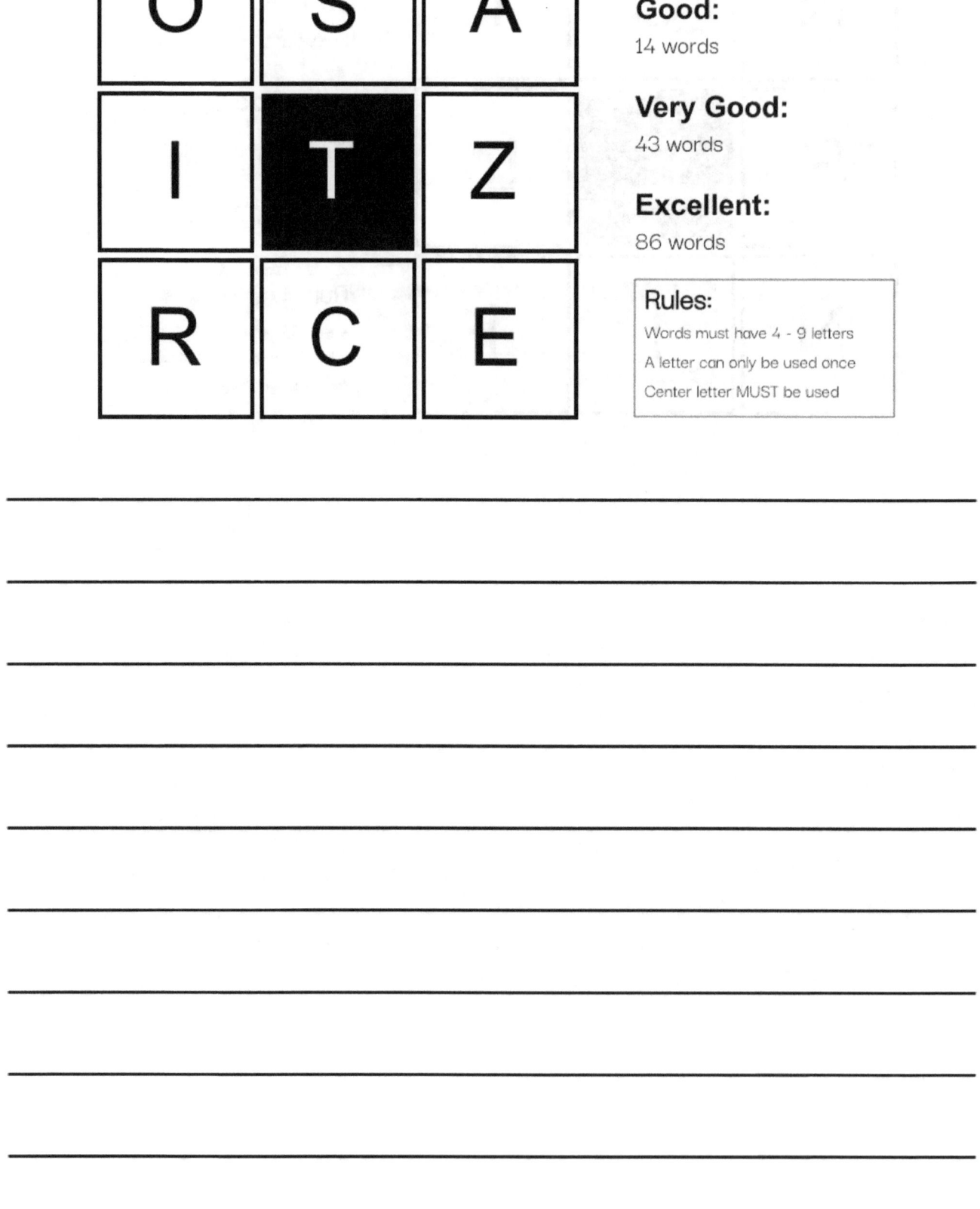

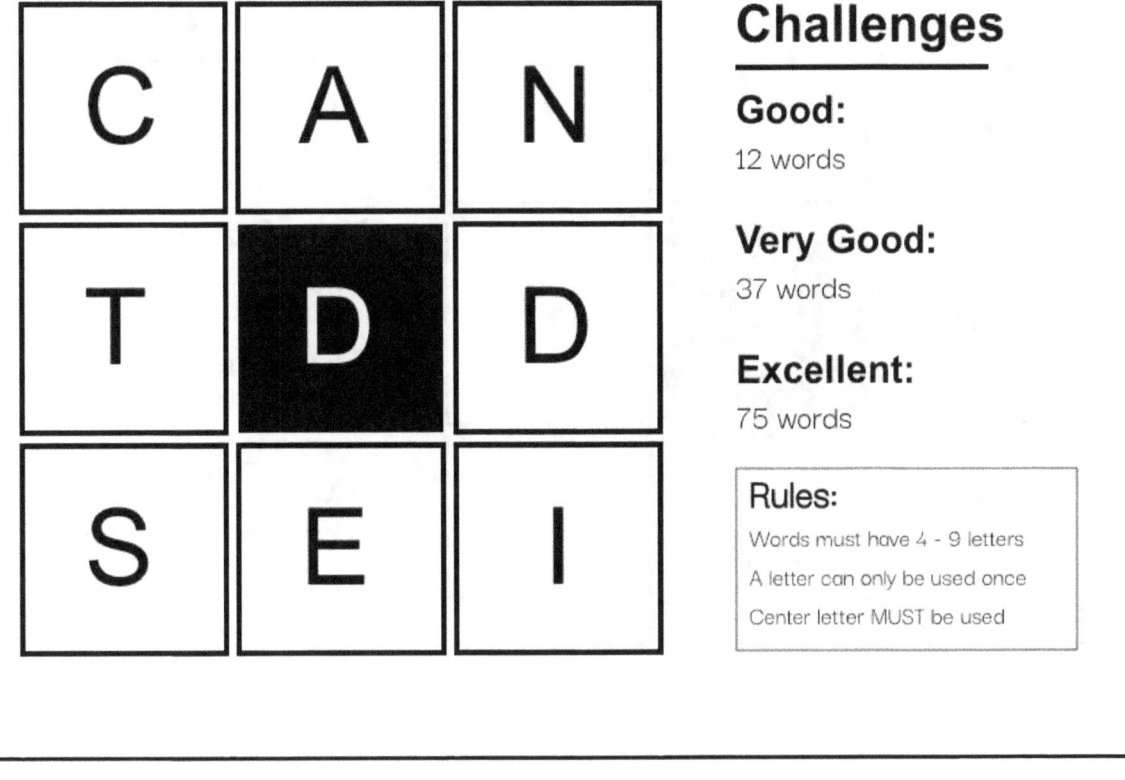

Challenges

Good:
2 words

Very Good:
7 words

Excellent:
15 words

Rules:
Words must have 4 - 9 letters
A letter can only be used once
Center letter MUST be used

48

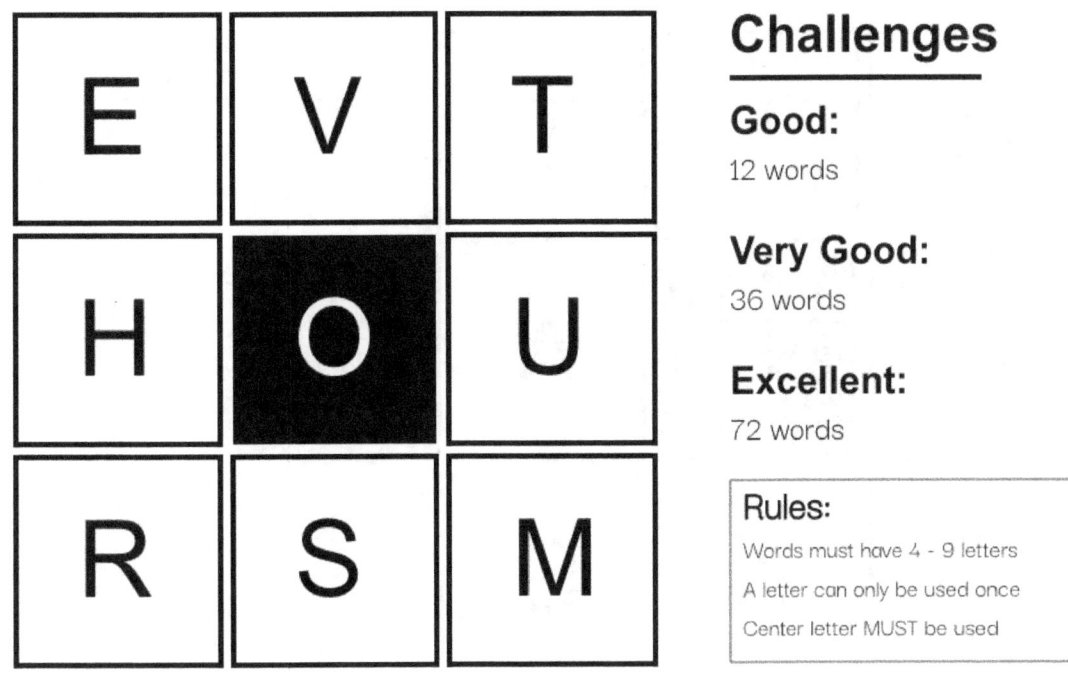

Challenges

Good:
12 words

Very Good:
36 words

Excellent:
72 words

Rules:
Words must have 4 - 9 letters
A letter can only be used once
Center letter MUST be used

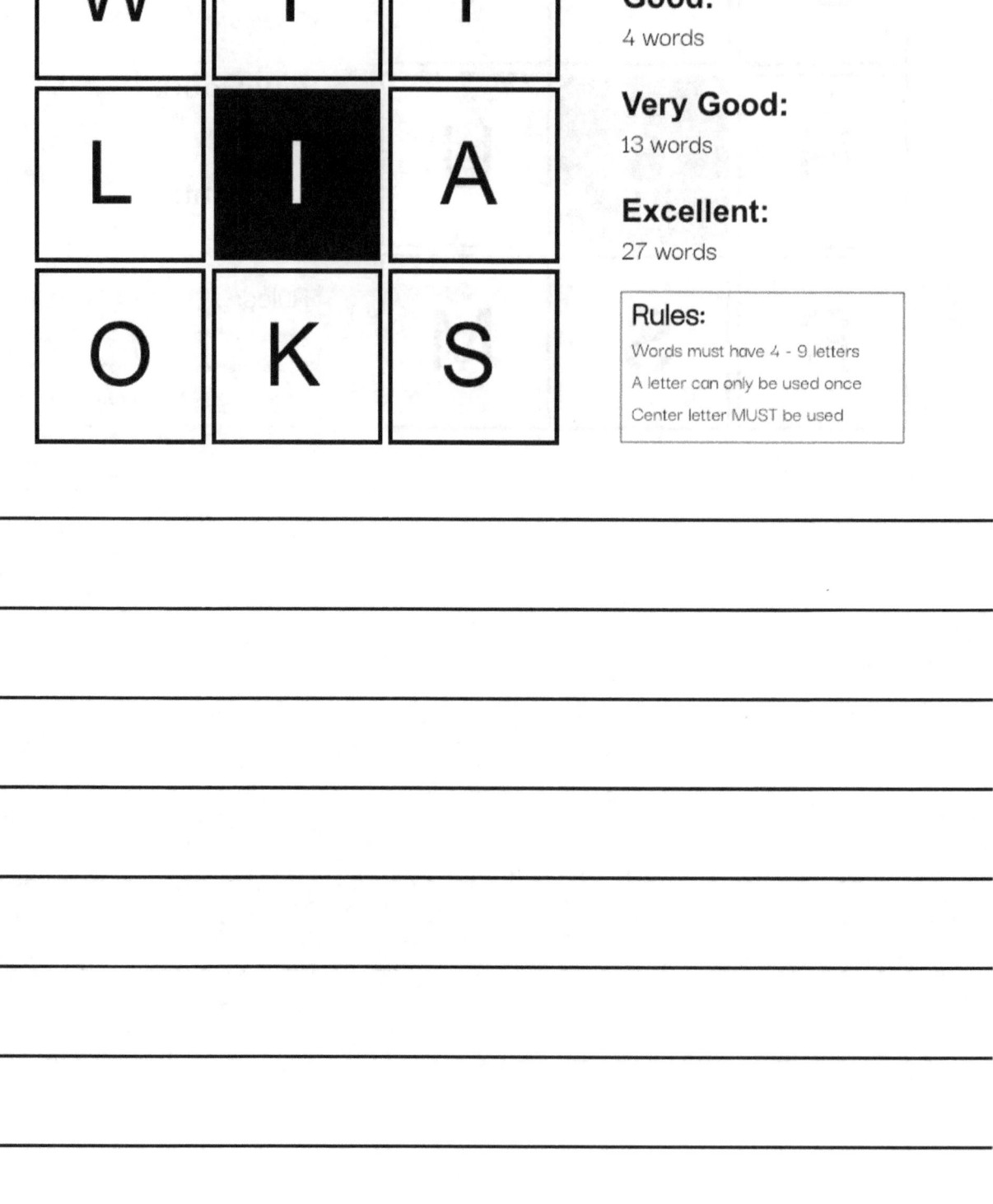

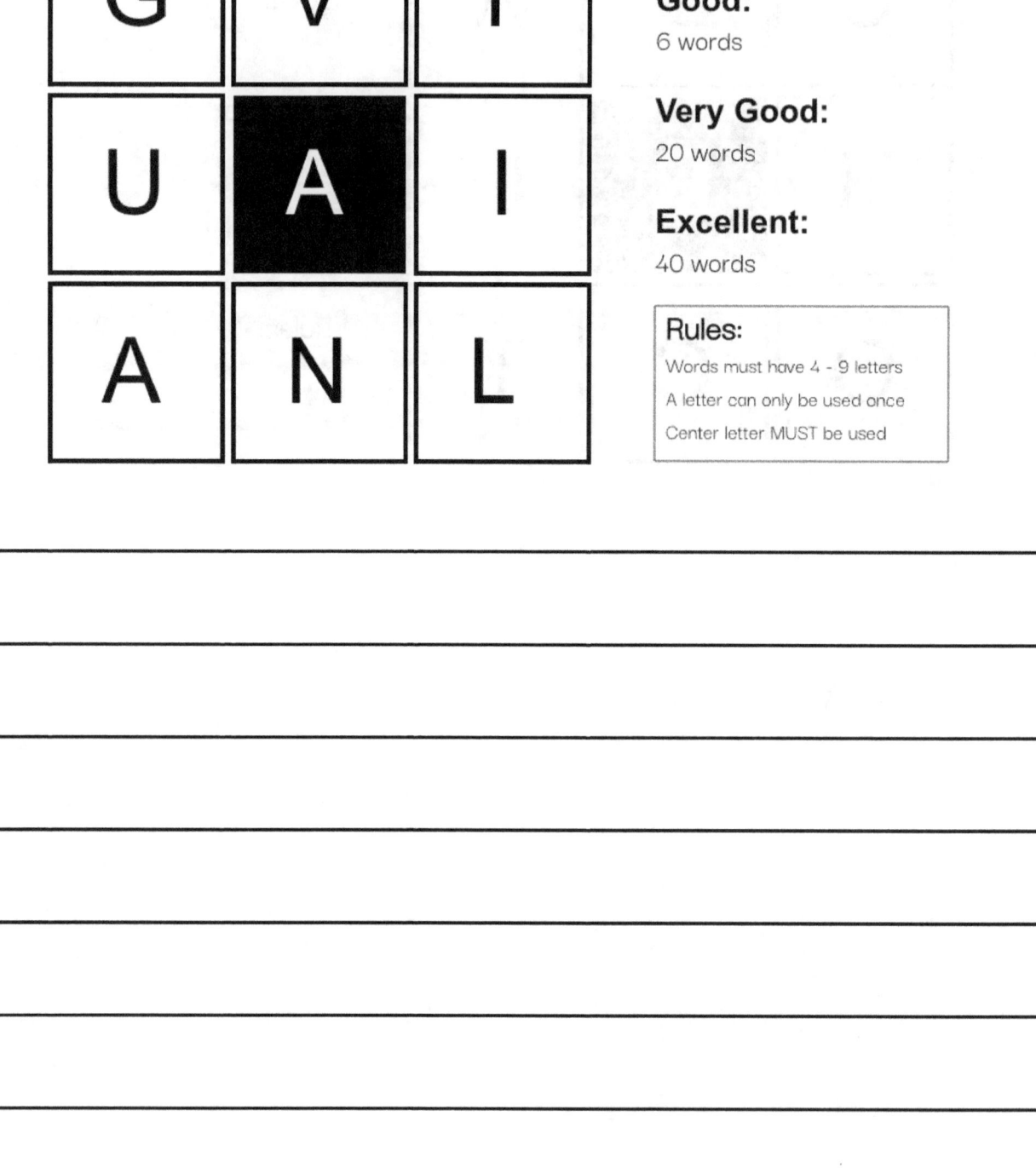

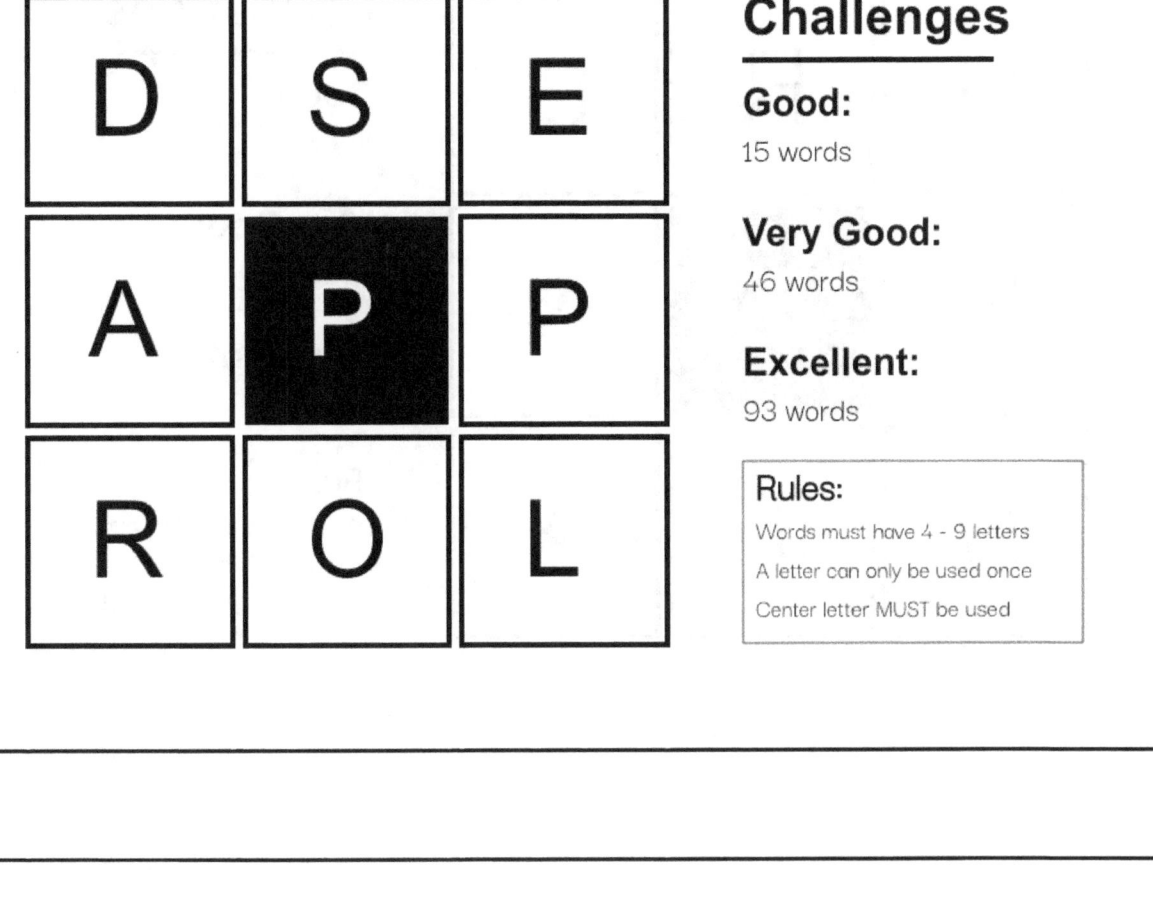

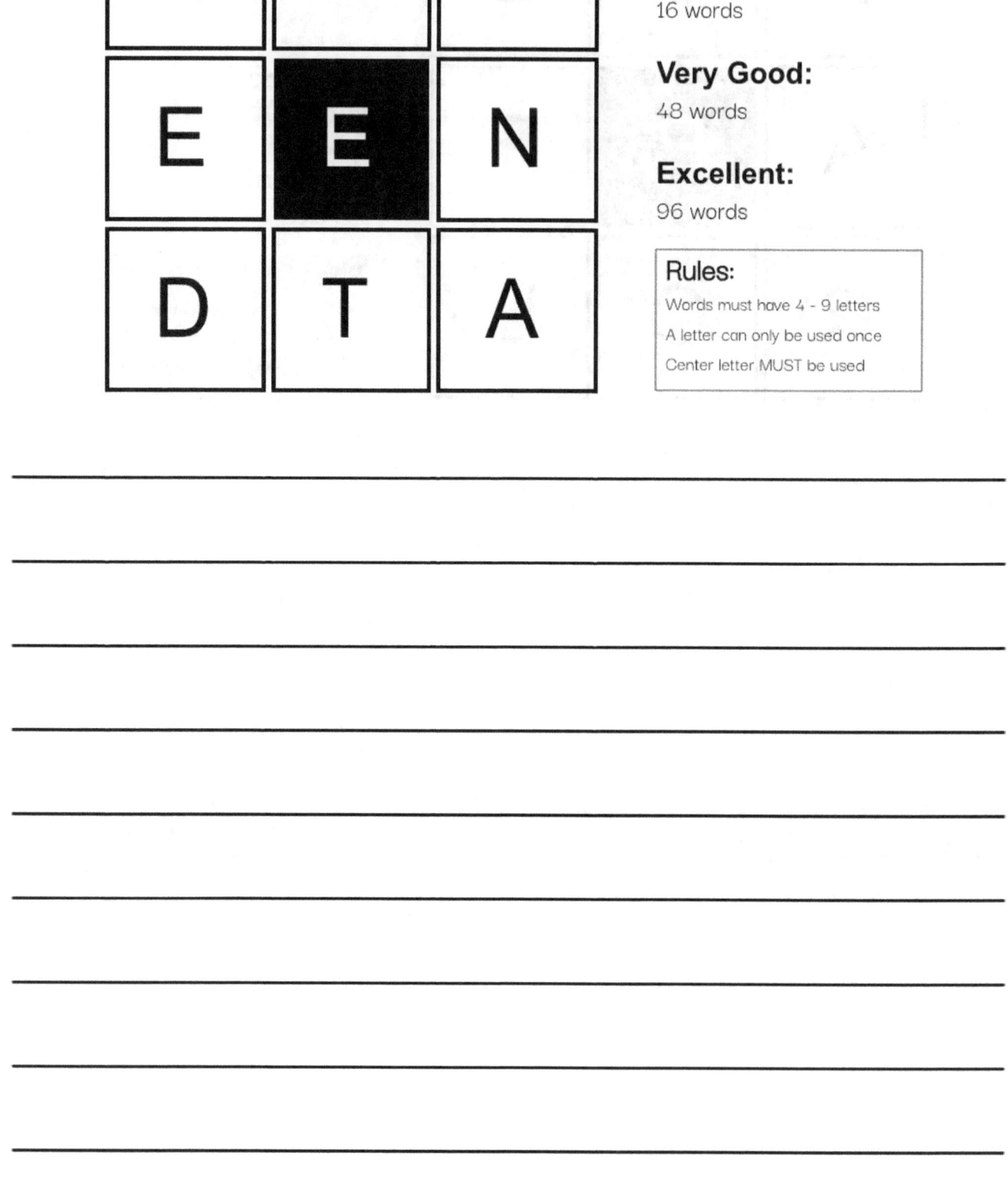

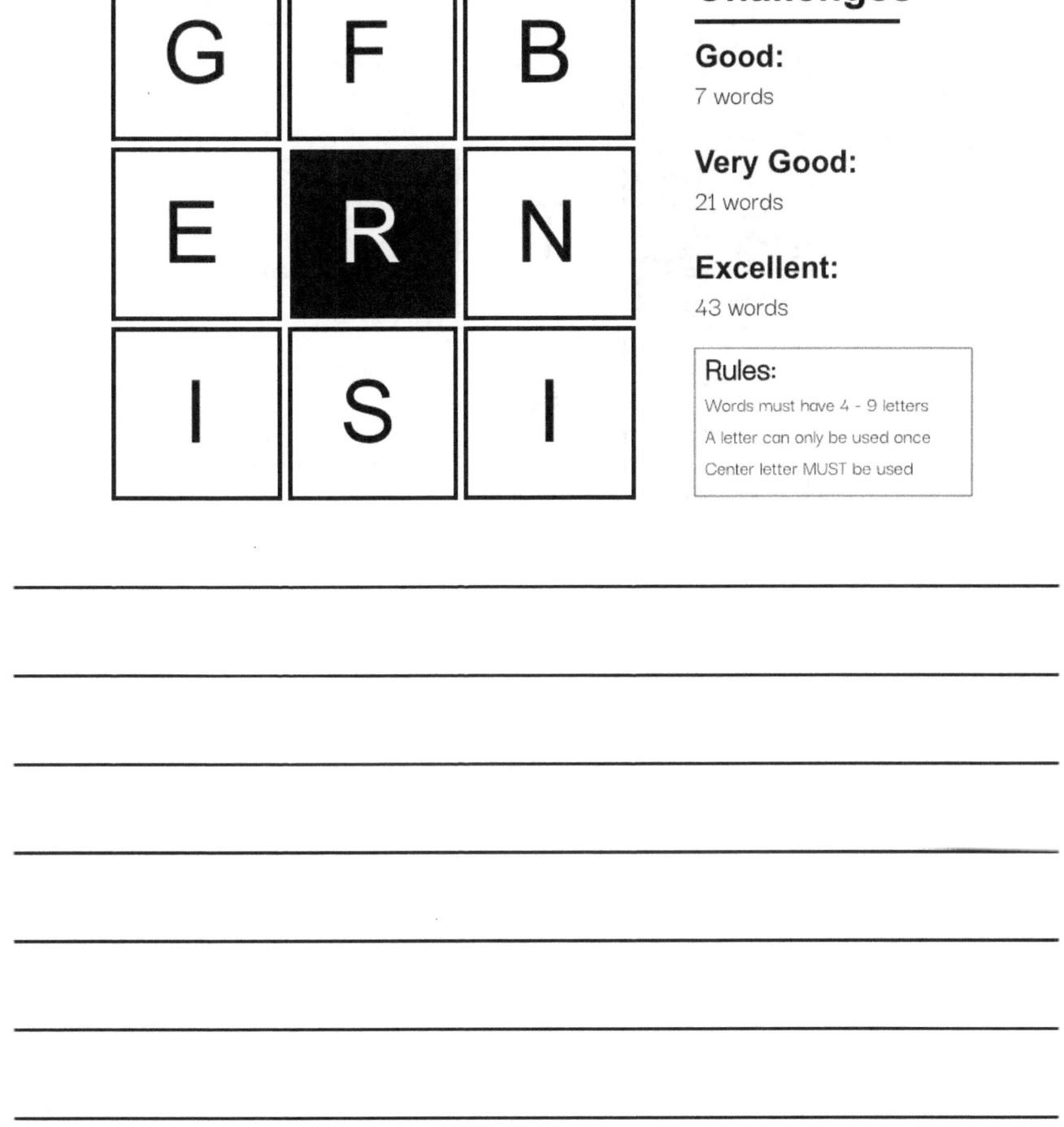

Challenges

Good:
6 words

Very Good:
19 words

Excellent:
39 words

Rules:
Words must have 4 - 9 letters
A letter can only be used once
Center letter MUST be used

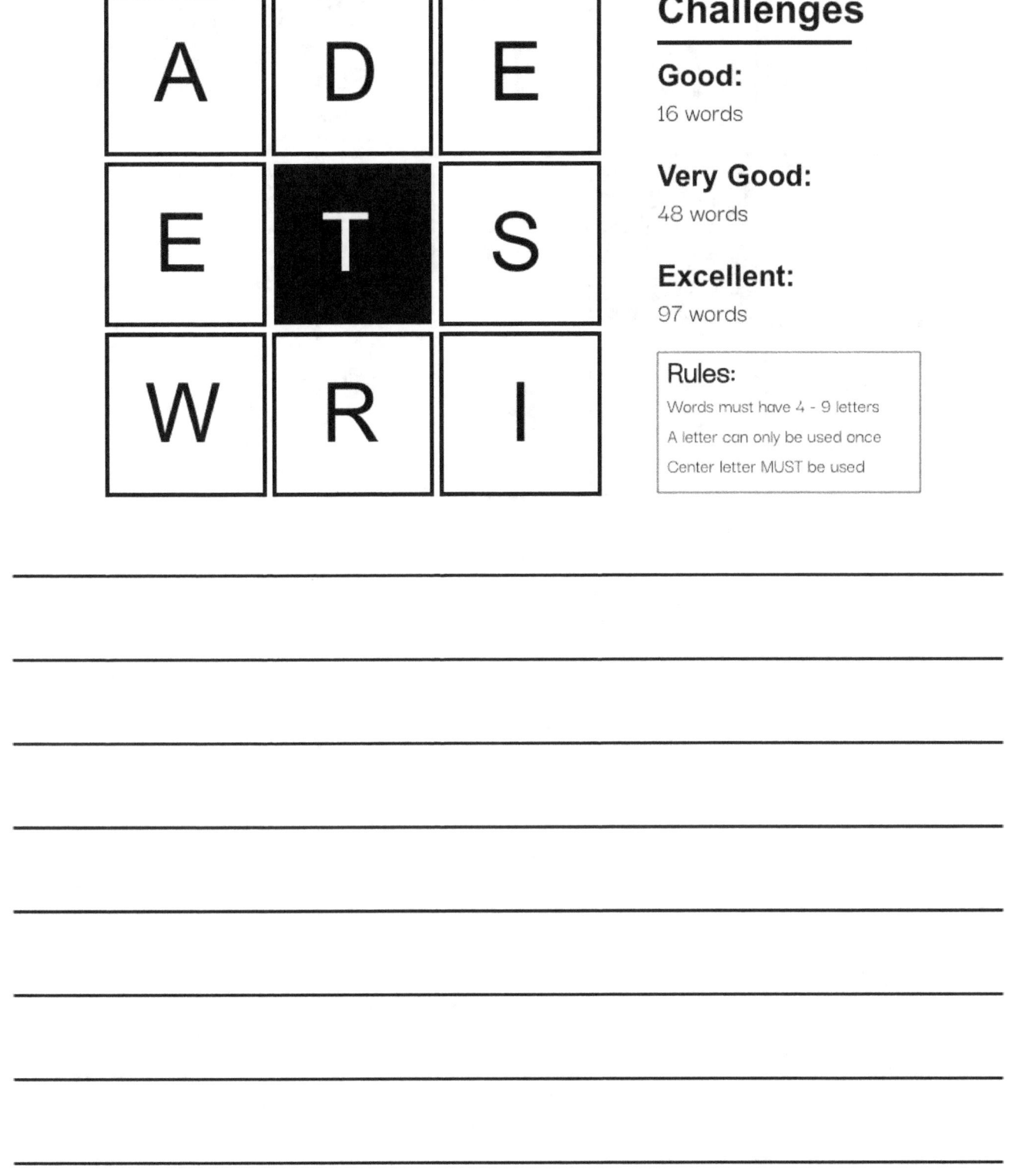

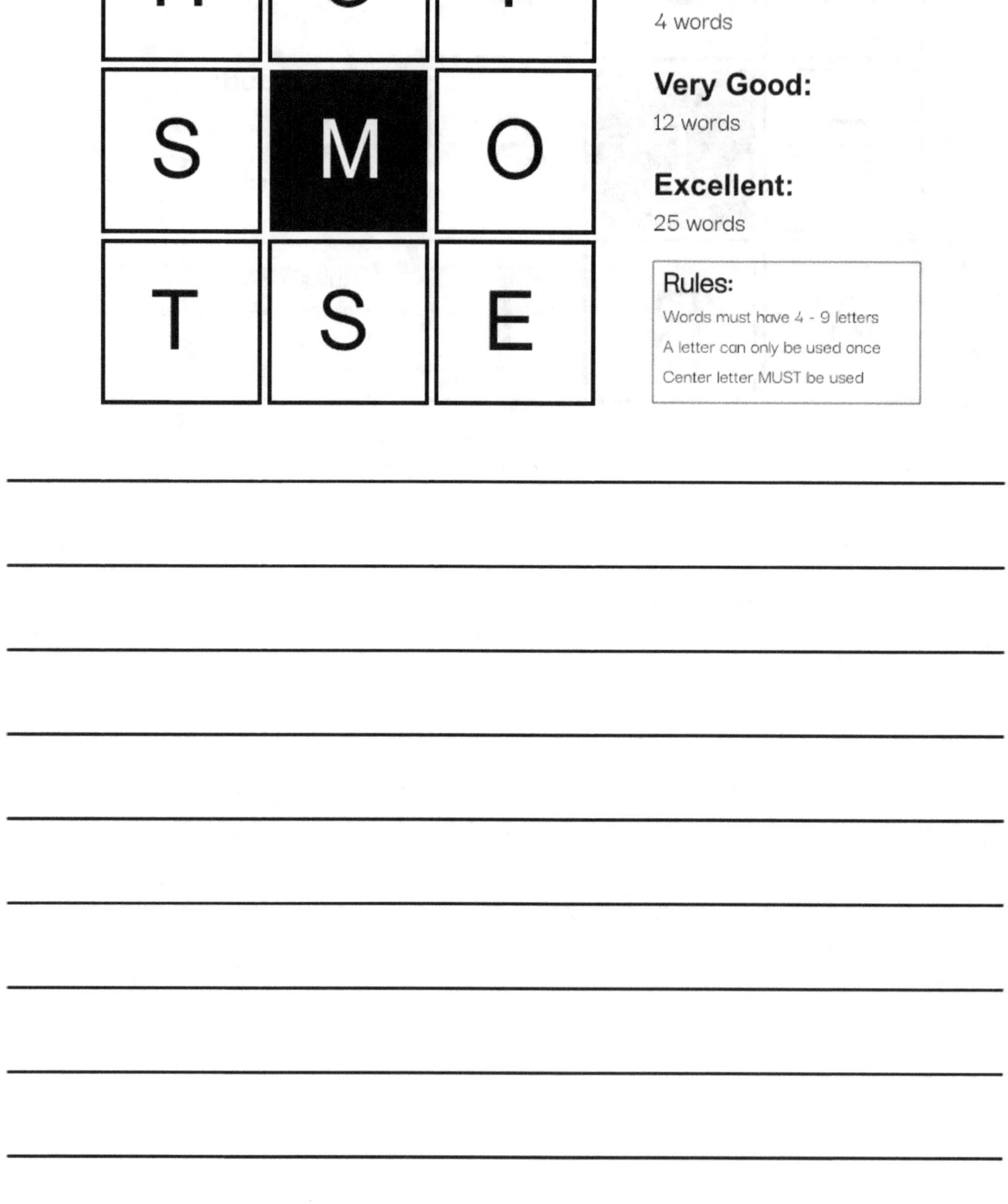

Challenges

Good:
1 words

Very Good:
3 words

Excellent:
7 words

Rules:
Words must have 4 - 9 letters
A letter can only be used once
Center letter MUST be used

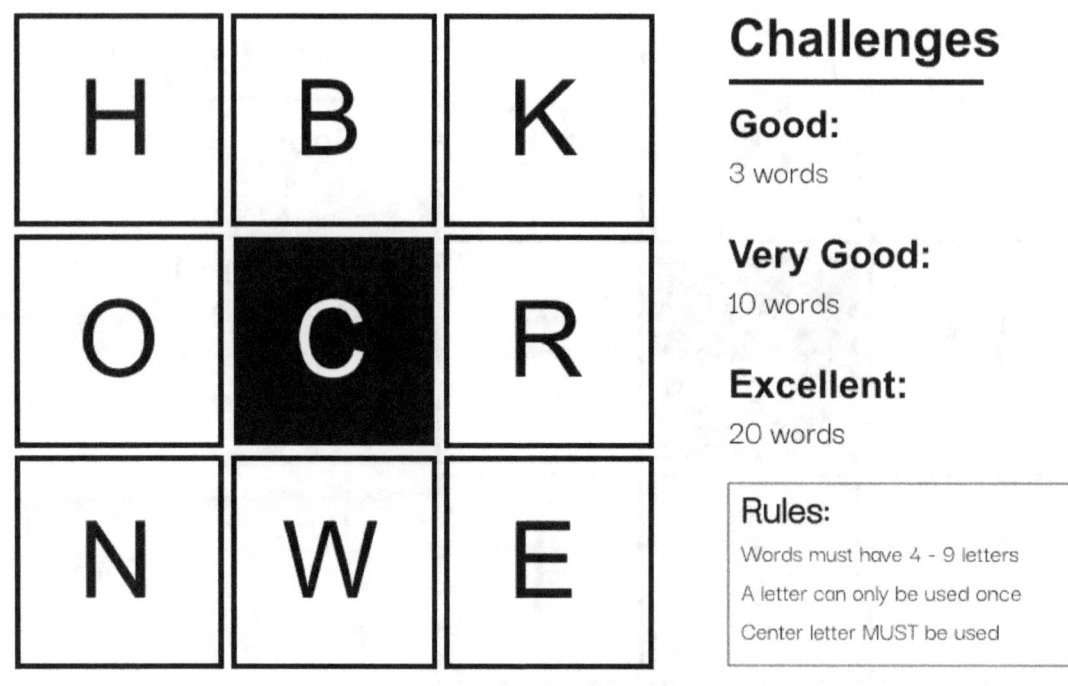

Challenges

Good:
3 words

Very Good:
10 words

Excellent:
20 words

Rules:
Words must have 4 - 9 letters
A letter can only be used once
Center letter MUST be used

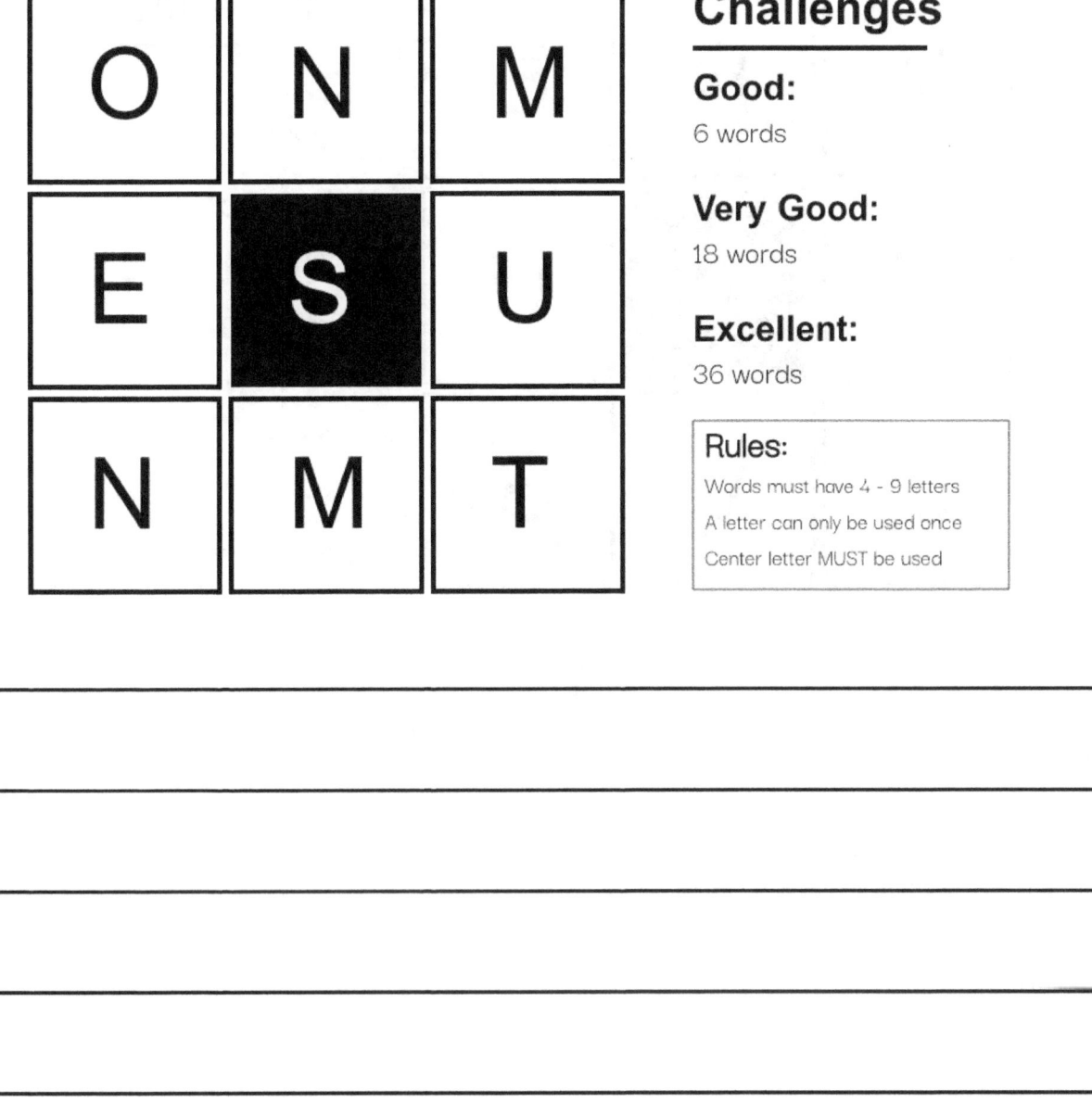

Challenges

Good:
6 words

Very Good:
18 words

Excellent:
36 words

Rules:
Words must have 4 - 9 letters
A letter can only be used once
Center letter MUST be used

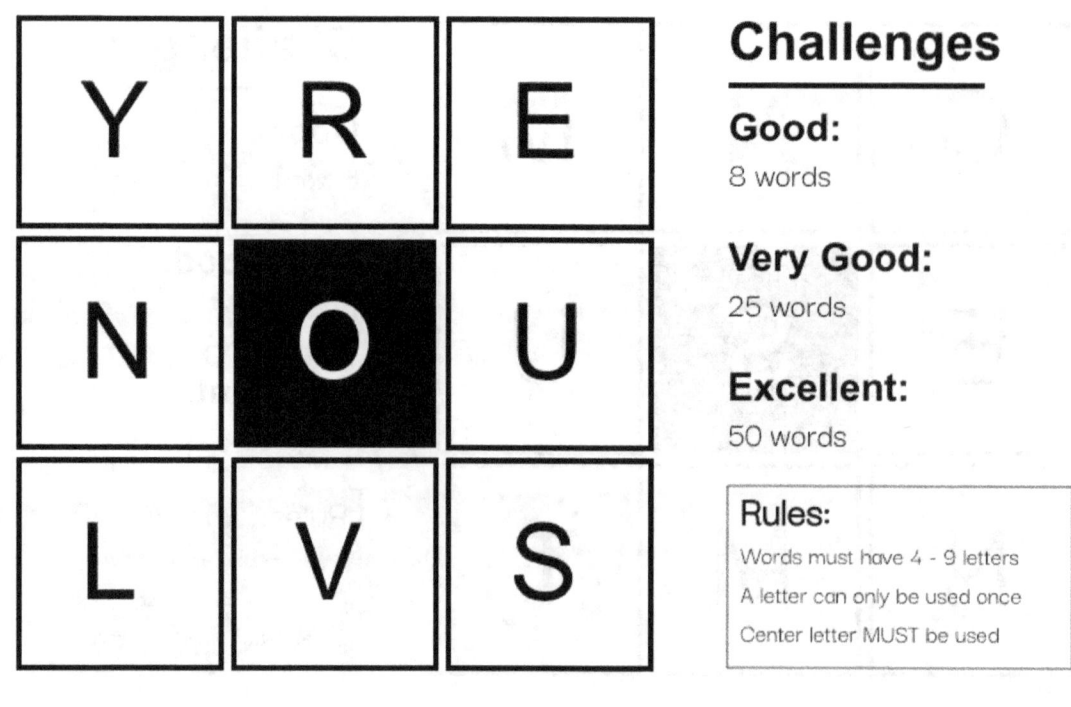

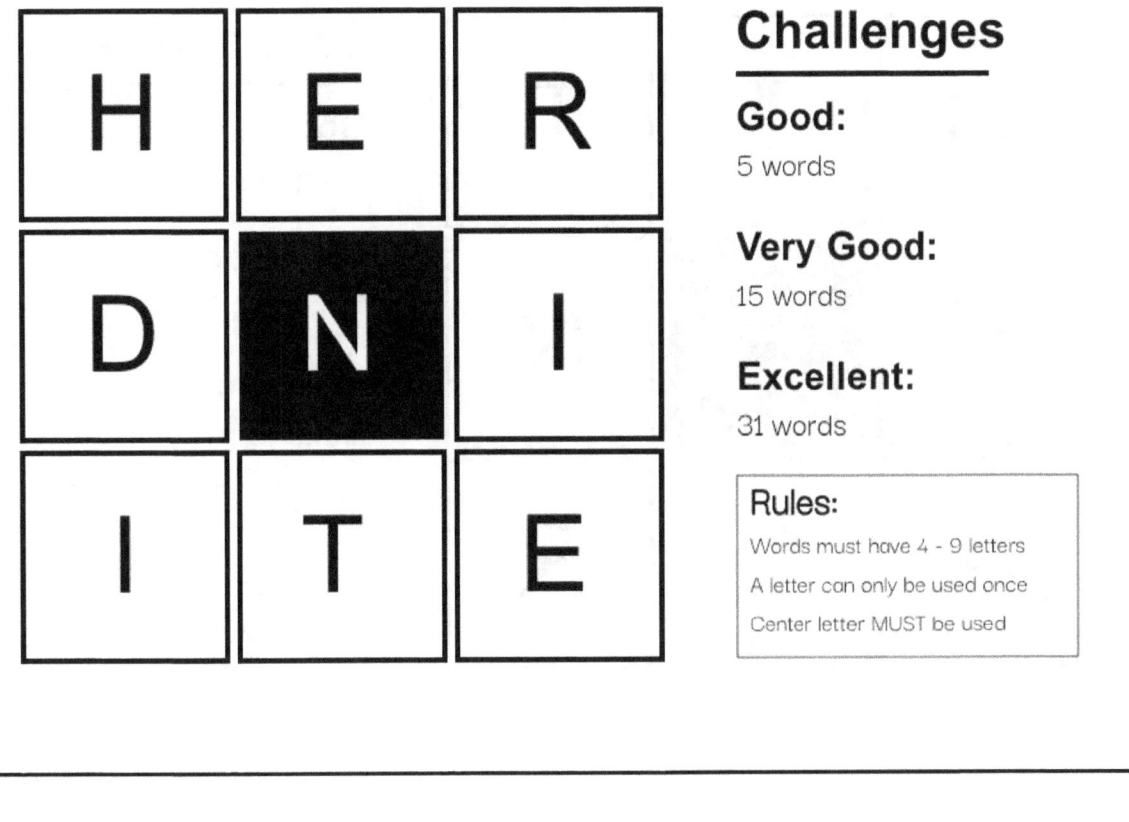

Challenges

Good:
5 words

Very Good:
15 words

Excellent:
31 words

Rules:
Words must have 4 - 9 letters
A letter can only be used once
Center letter MUST be used

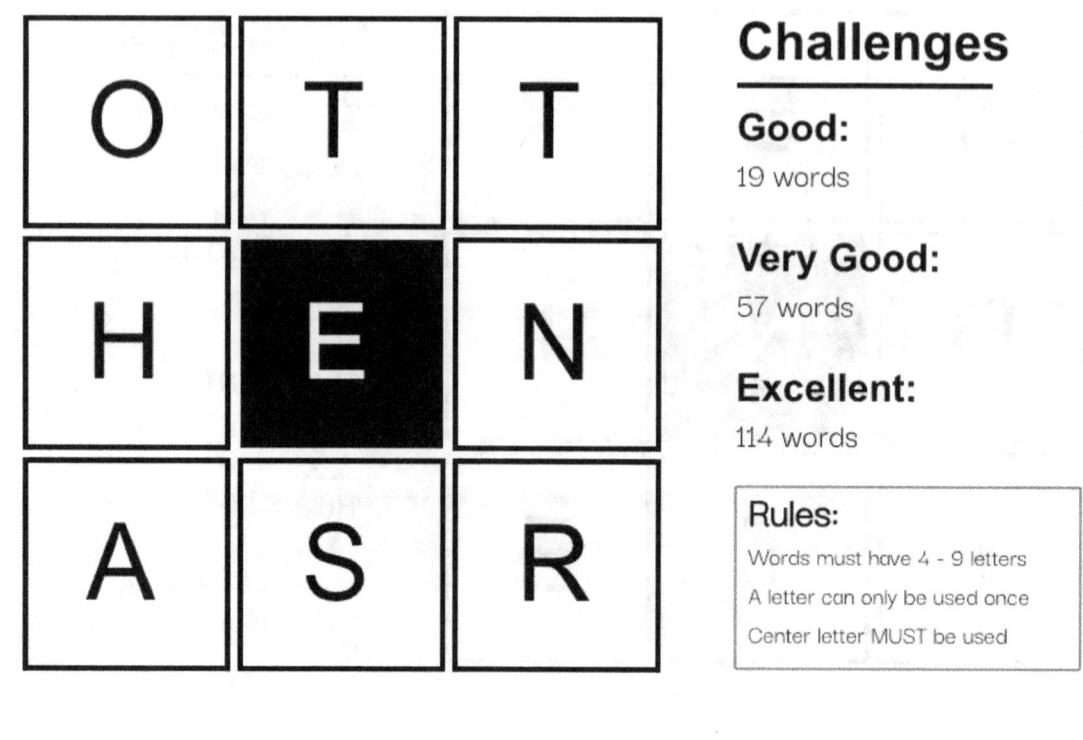

Challenges

Good:
19 words

Very Good:
57 words

Excellent:
114 words

Rules:
Words must have 4 - 9 letters
A letter can only be used once
Center letter MUST be used

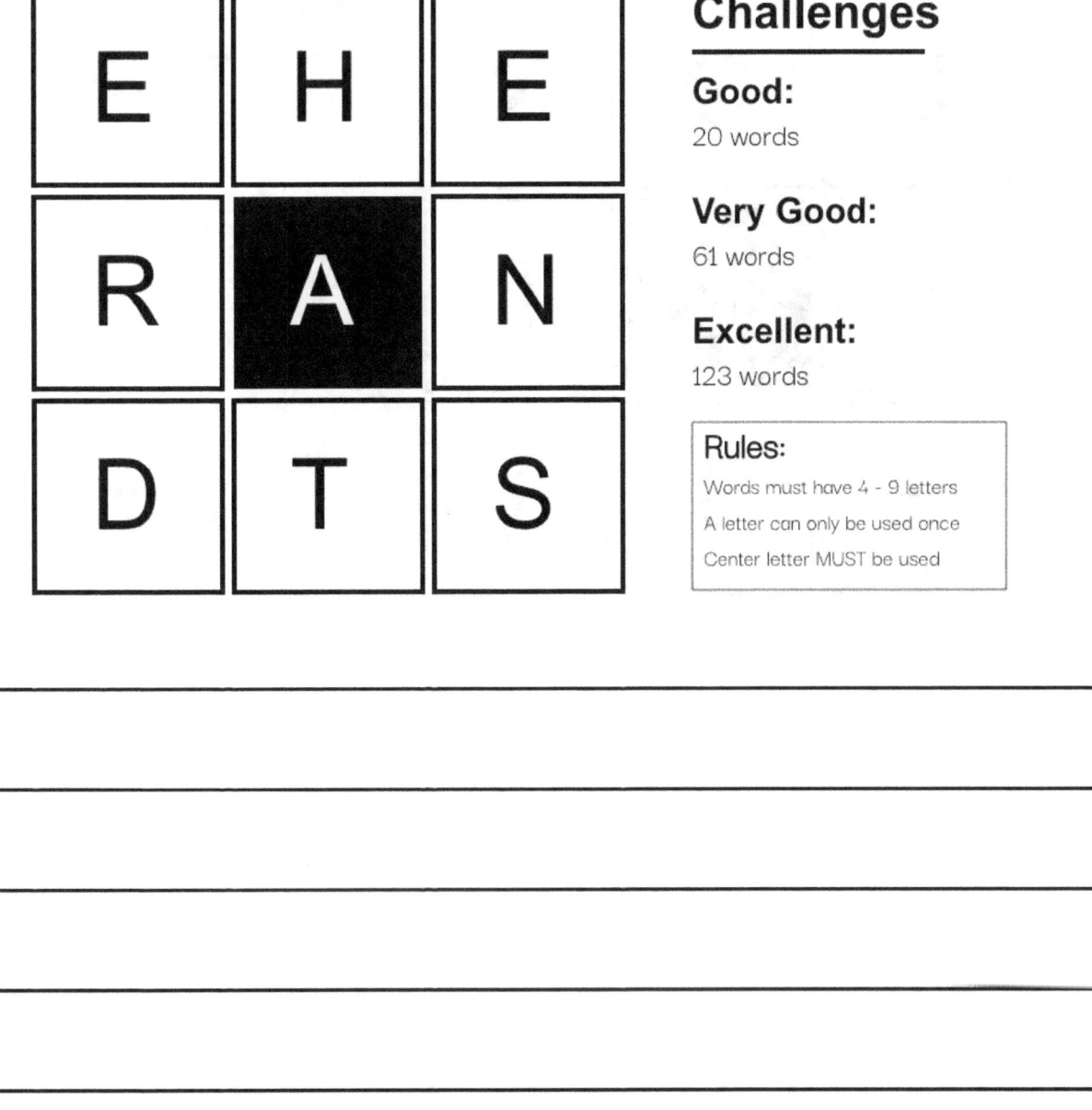

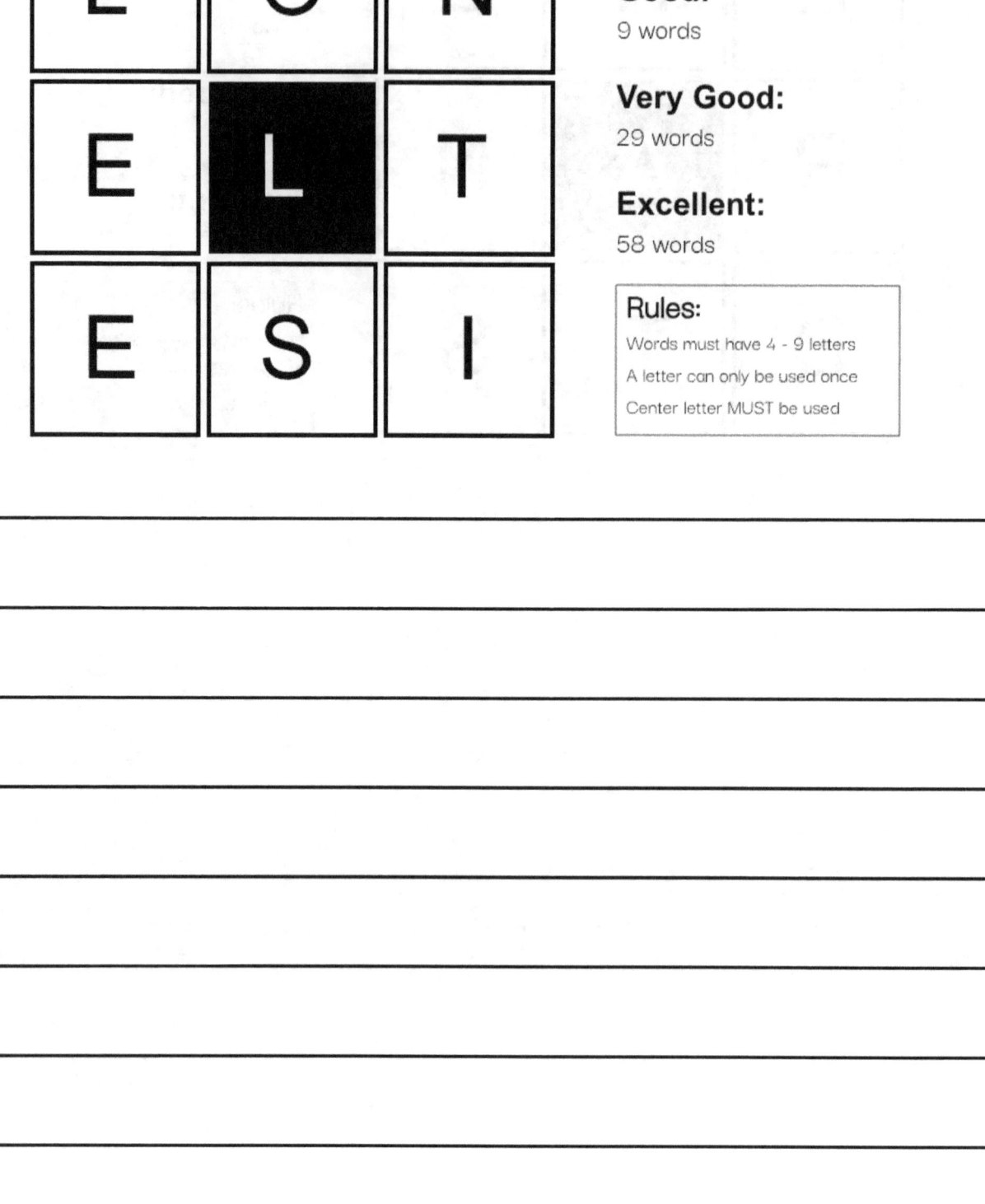

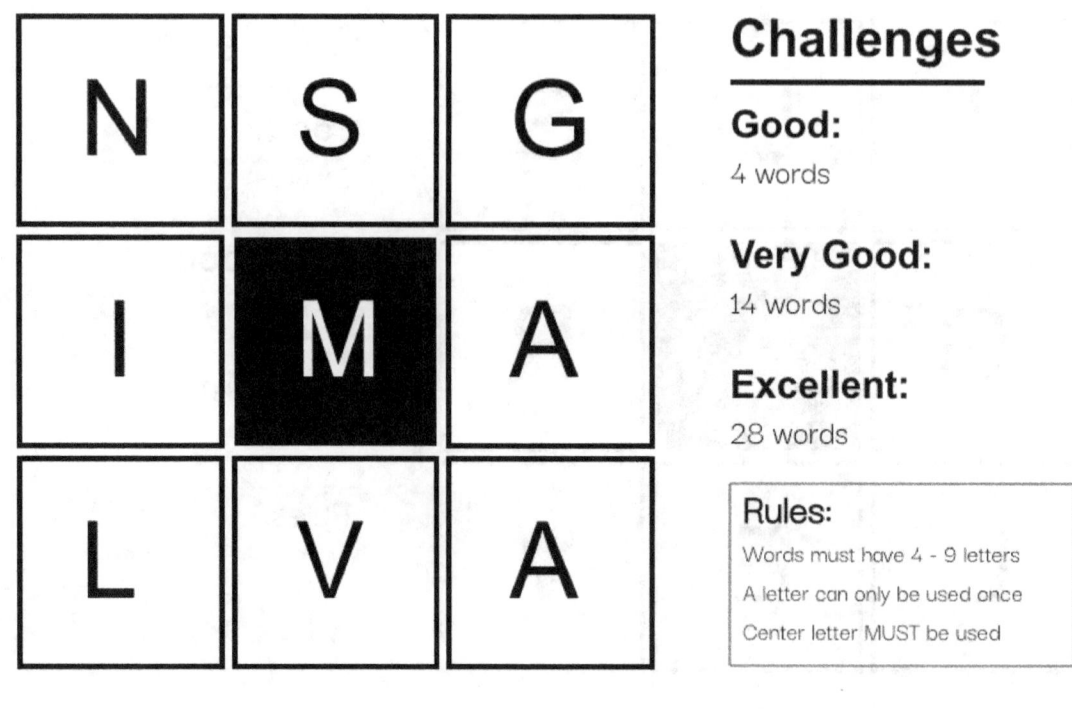

Challenges

Good:
4 words

Very Good:
14 words

Excellent:
28 words

Rules:
Words must have 4 - 9 letters
A letter can only be used once
Center letter MUST be used

Challenges

Good:
13 words

Very Good:
41 words

Excellent:
82 words

Rules:
Words must have 4 - 9 letters
A letter can only be used once
Center letter MUST be used

R	A	D
S	**D**	N
O	L	L

Challenges

Good:
4 words

Very Good:
13 words

Excellent:
26 words

Rules:
Words must have 4 - 9 letters
A letter can only be used once
Center letter MUST be used

75

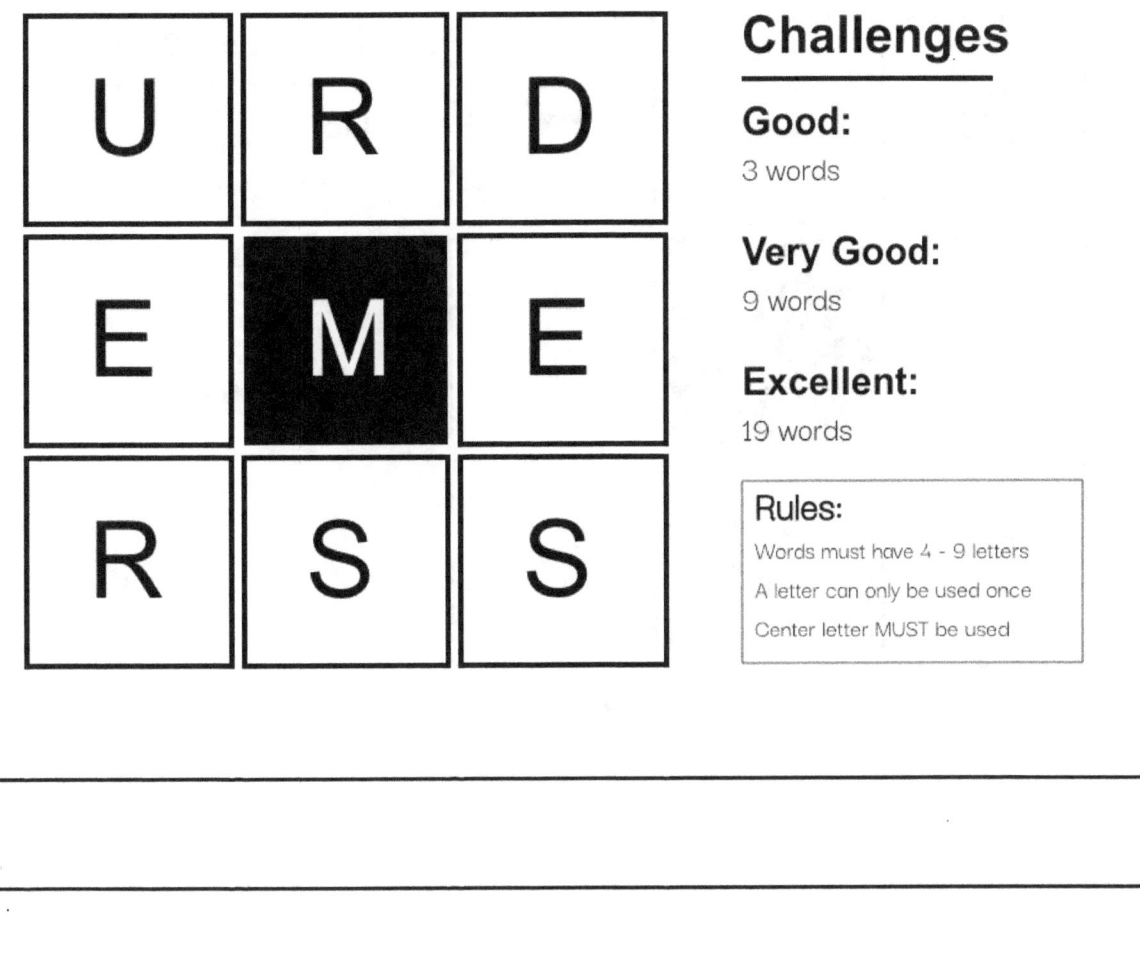

Challenges

Good:
3 words

Very Good:
9 words

Excellent:
19 words

Rules:
Words must have 4 - 9 letters
A letter can only be used once
Center letter MUST be used

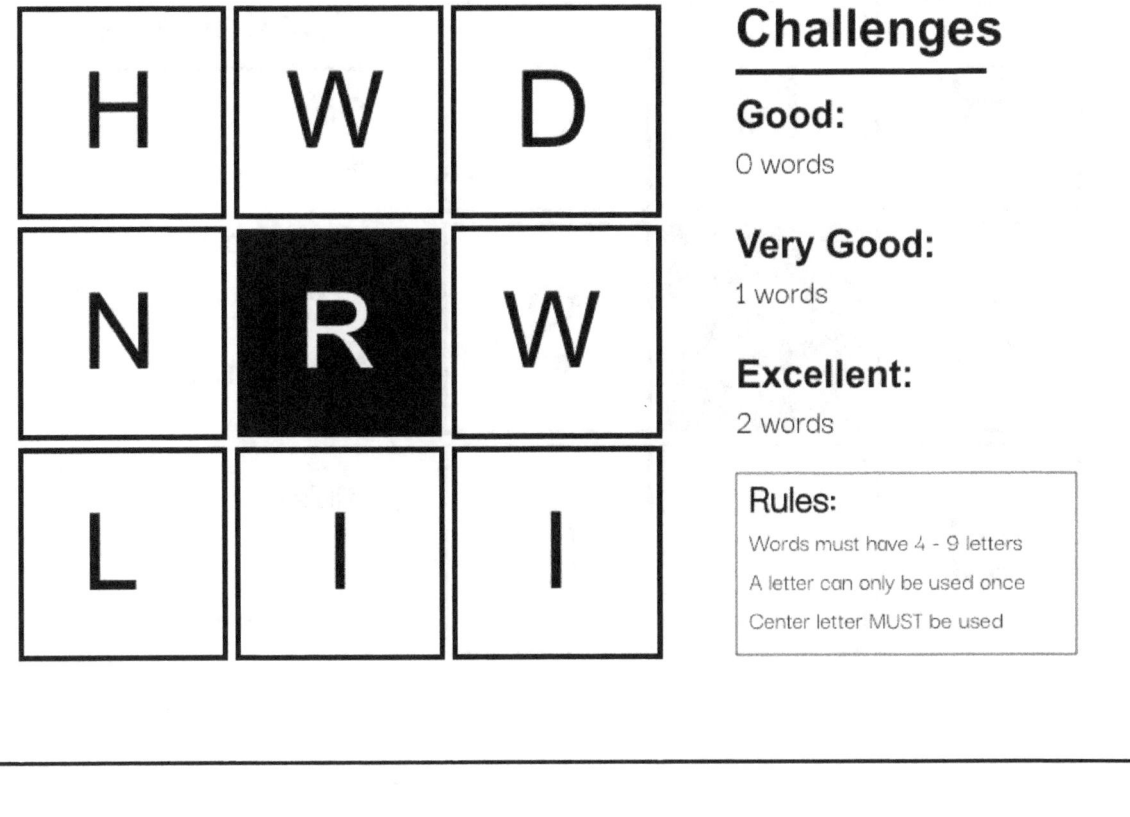

Challenges

Good:
0 words

Very Good:
1 words

Excellent:
2 words

Rules:
Words must have 4 - 9 letters
A letter can only be used once
Center letter MUST be used

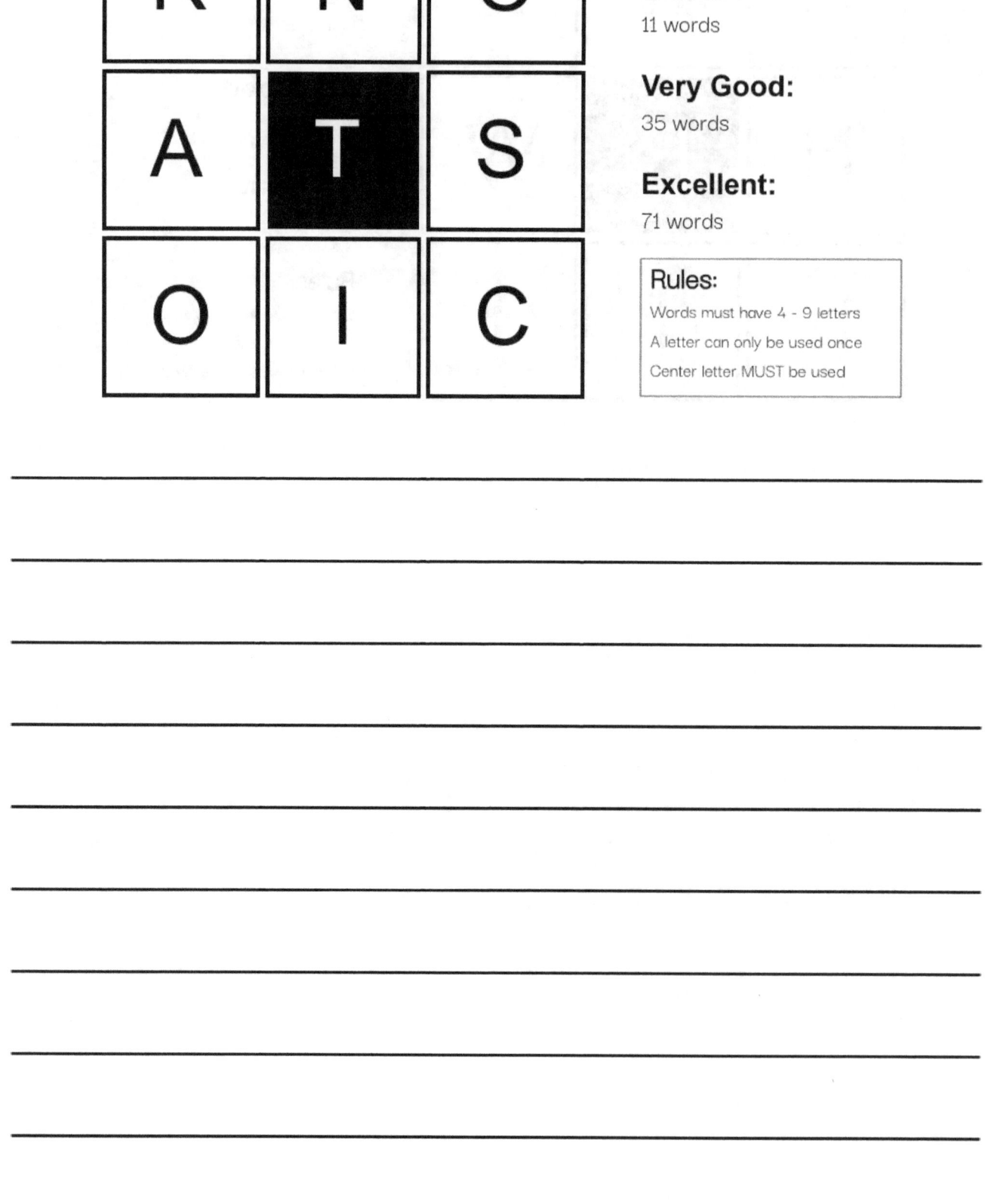

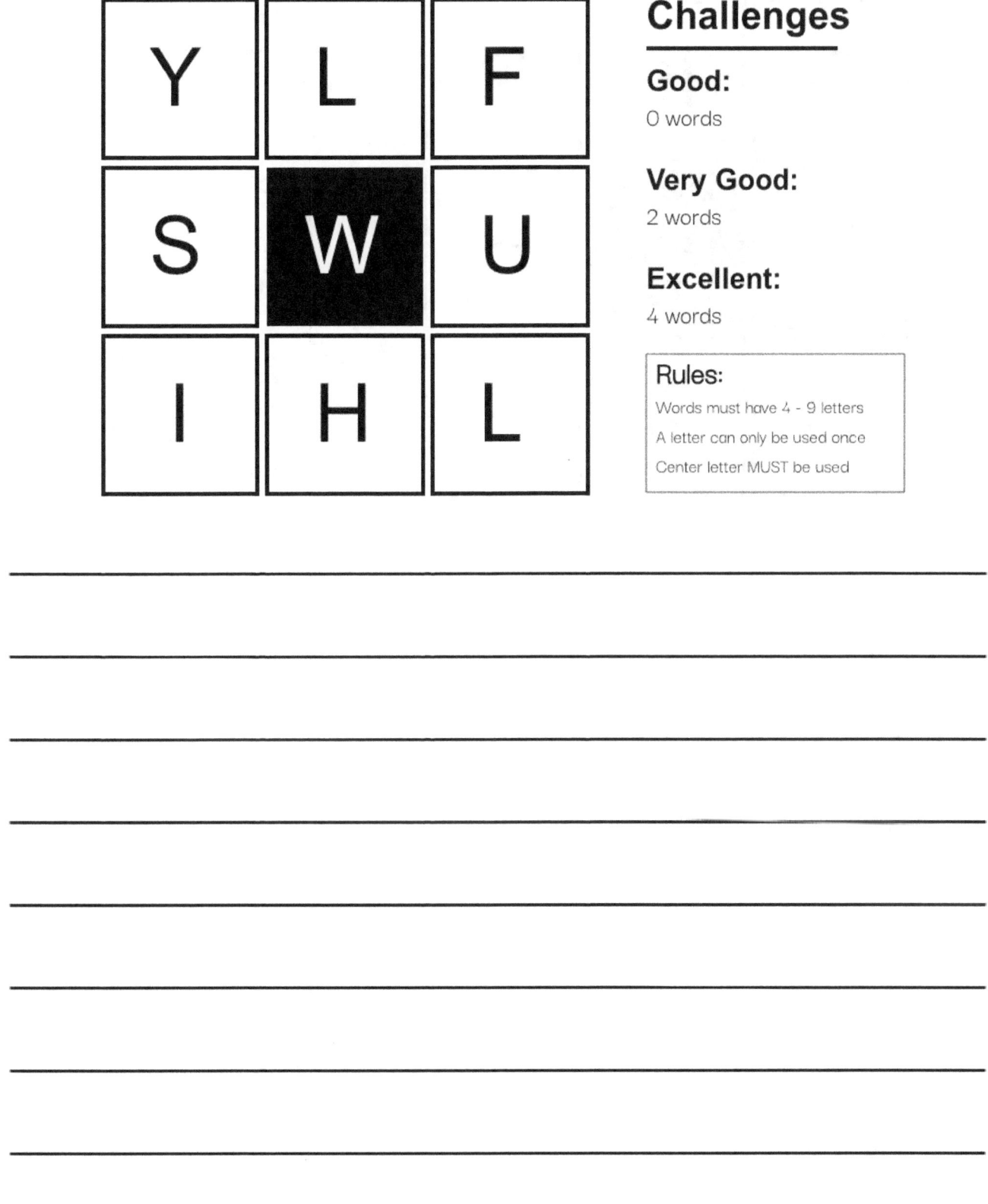

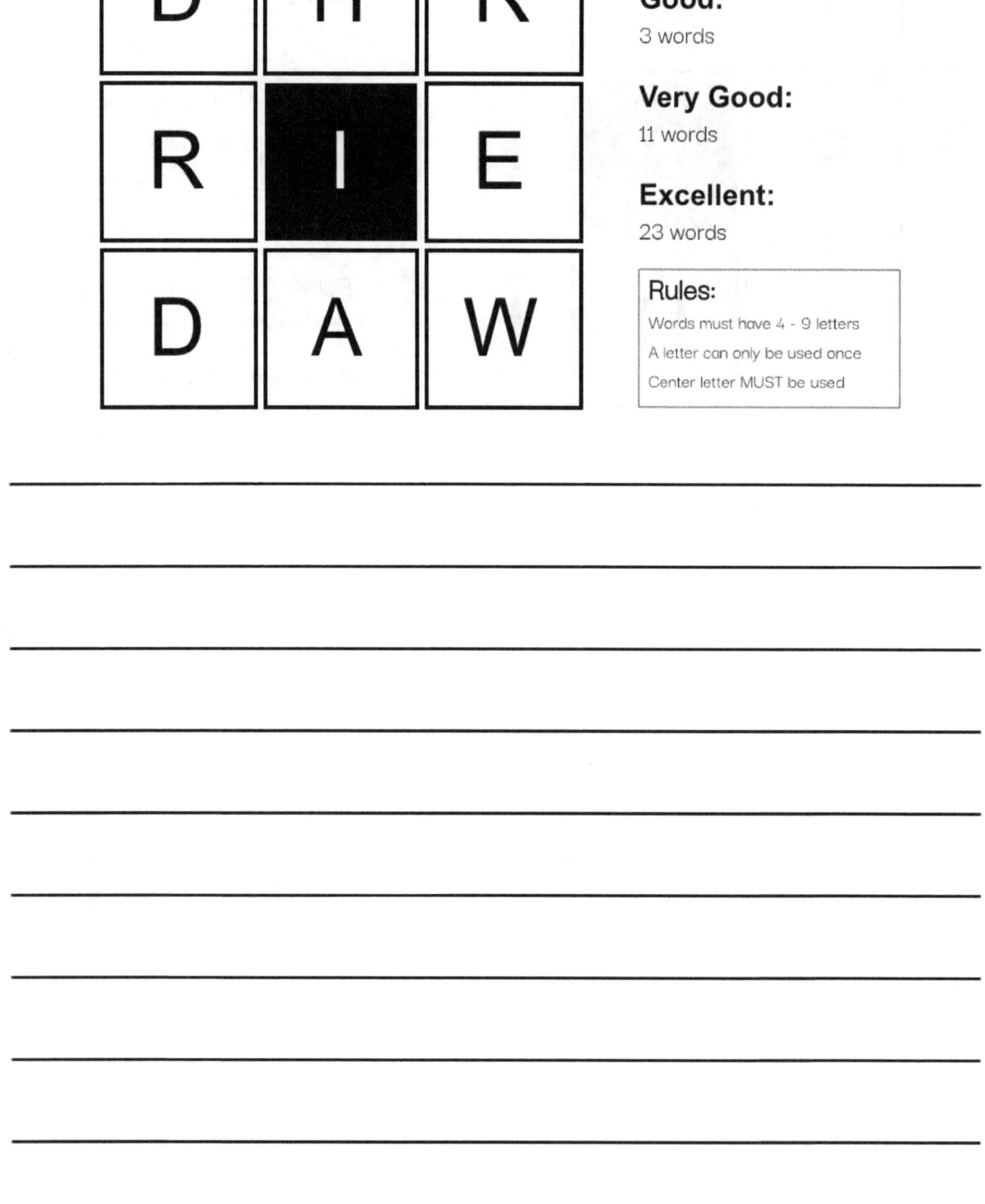

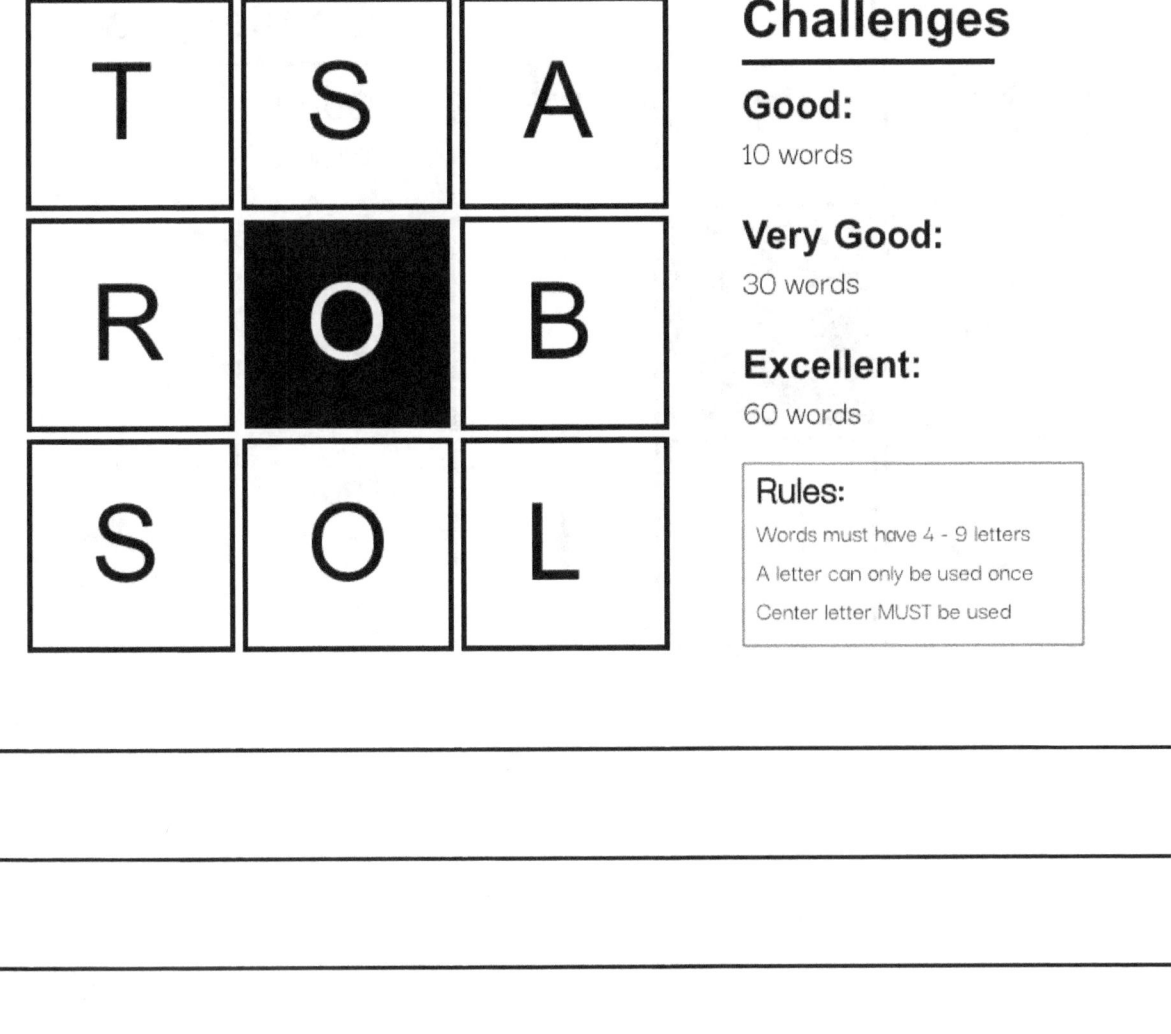

Challenges

Good:
10 words

Very Good:
30 words

Excellent:
60 words

Rules:
Words must have 4 - 9 letters
A letter can only be used once
Center letter MUST be used

83

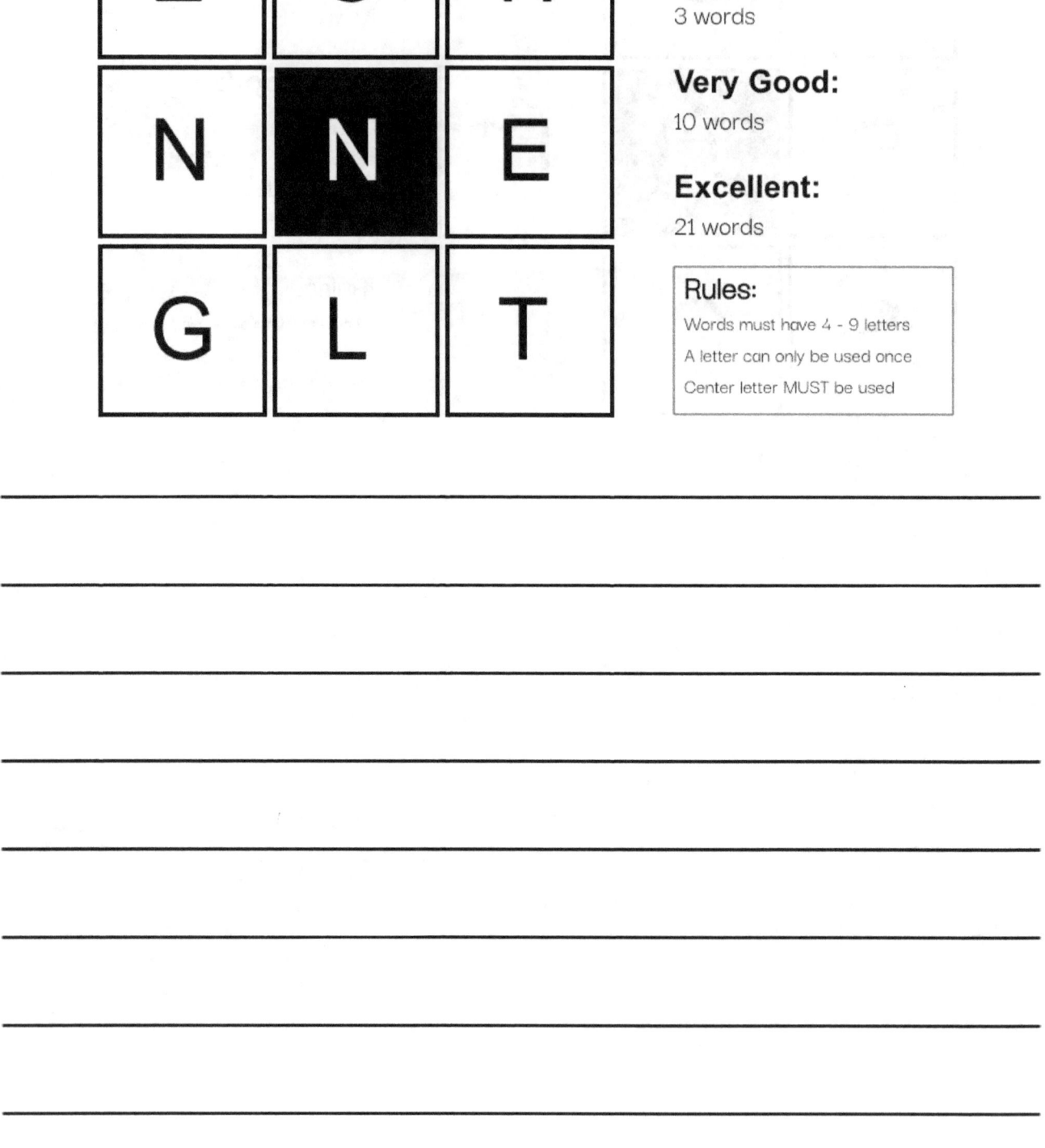

Challenges

Good:
8 words

Very Good:
25 words

Excellent:
51 words

Rules:
Words must have 4 - 9 letters
A letter can only be used once
Center letter MUST be used

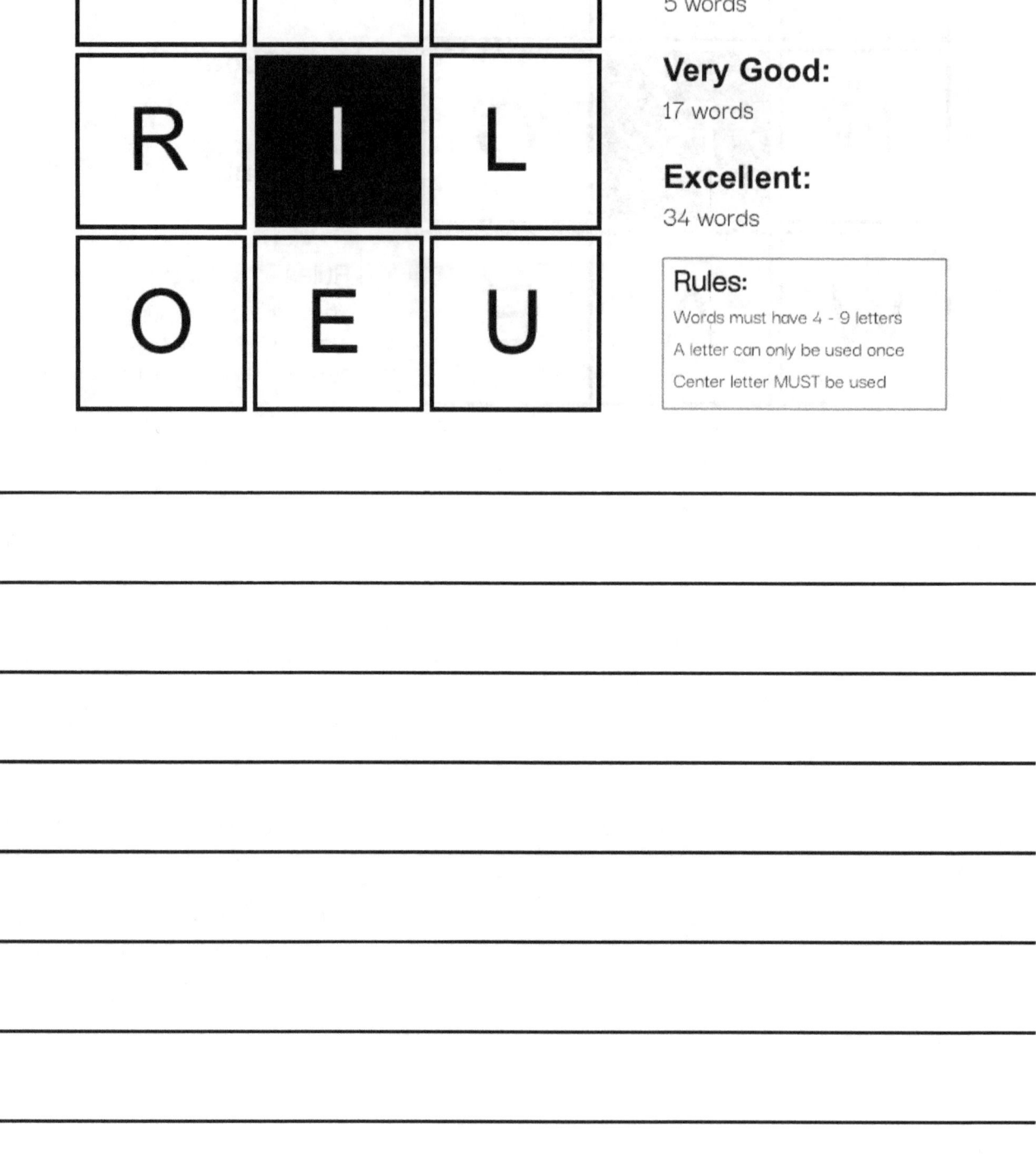

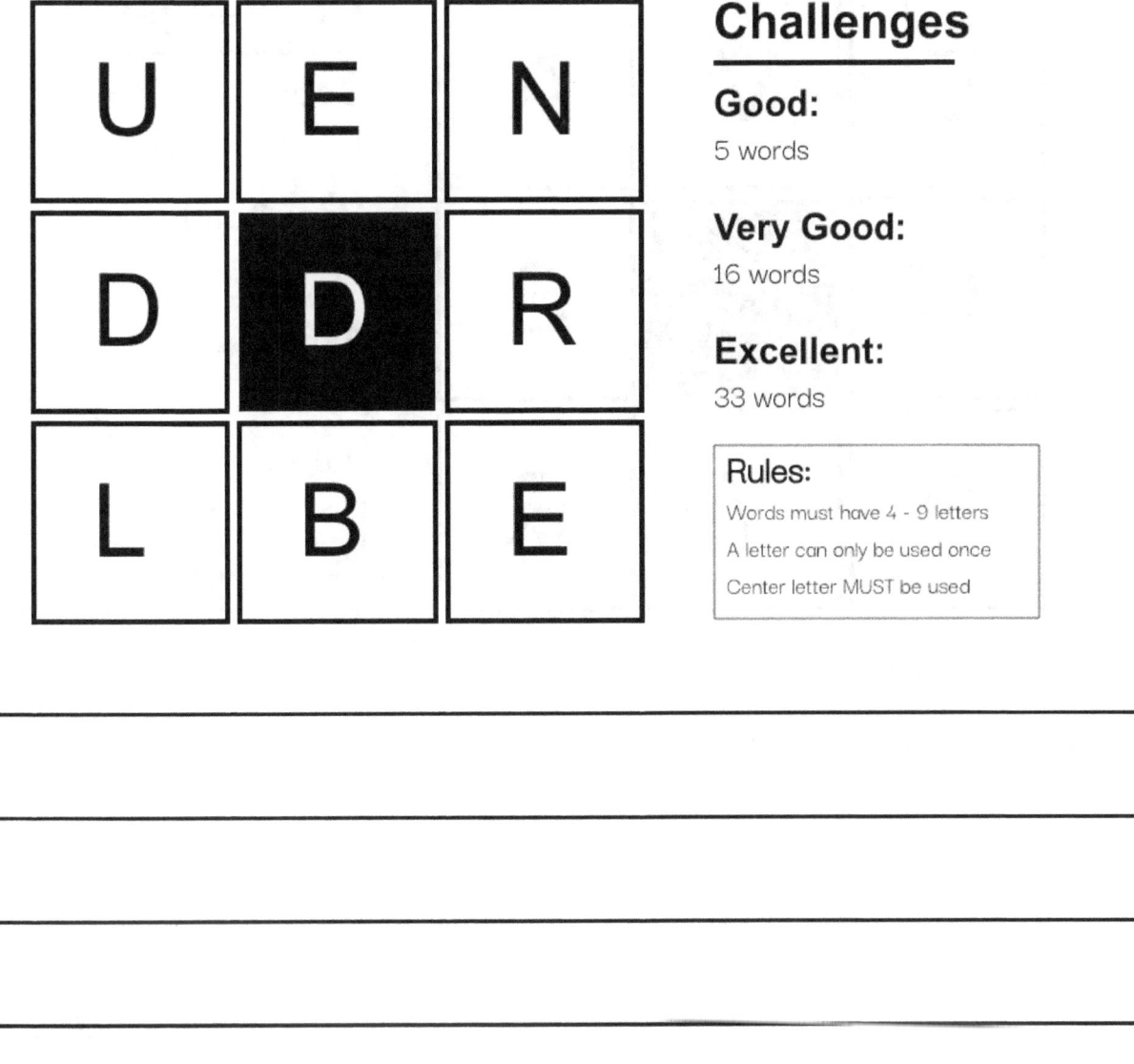

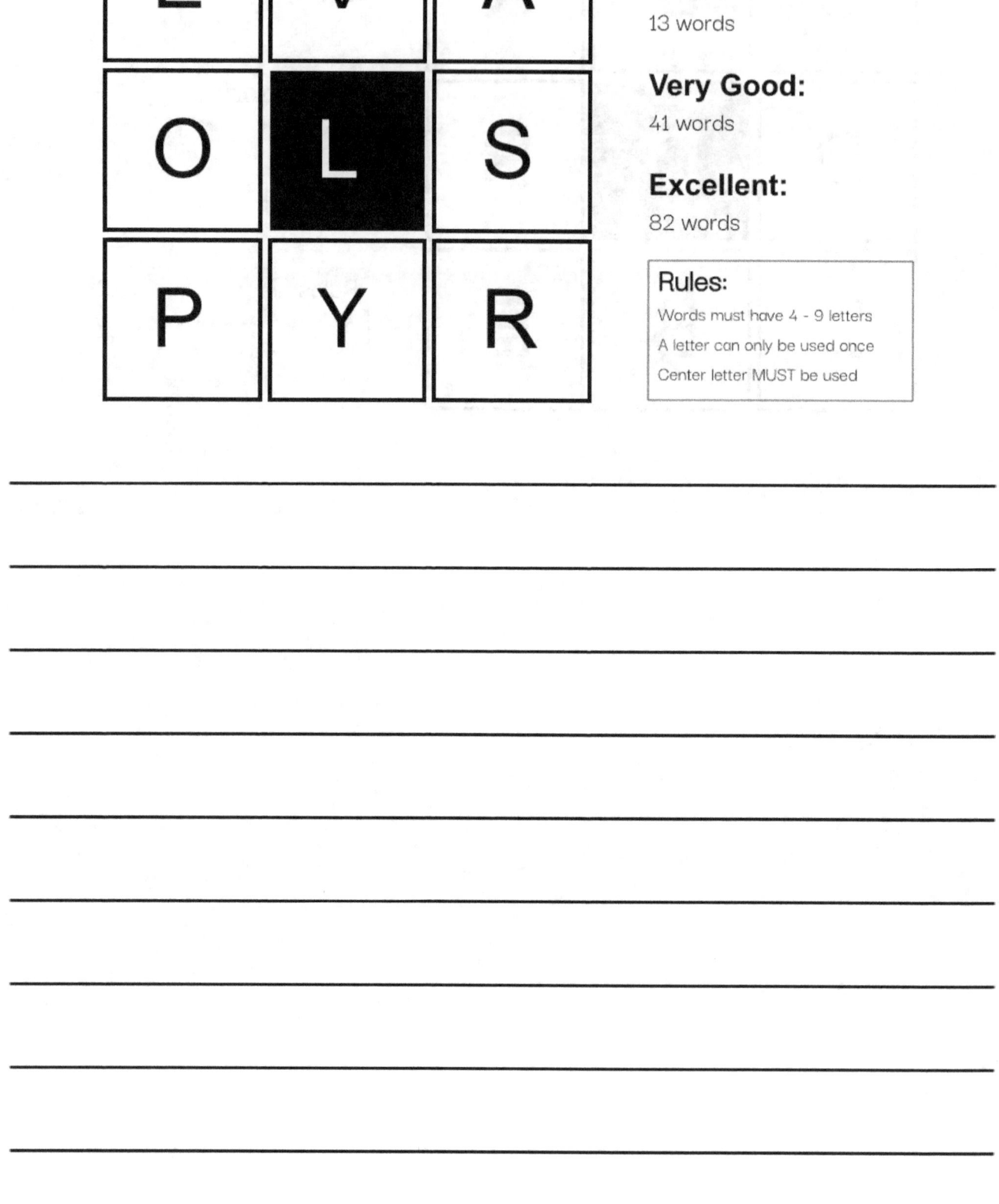

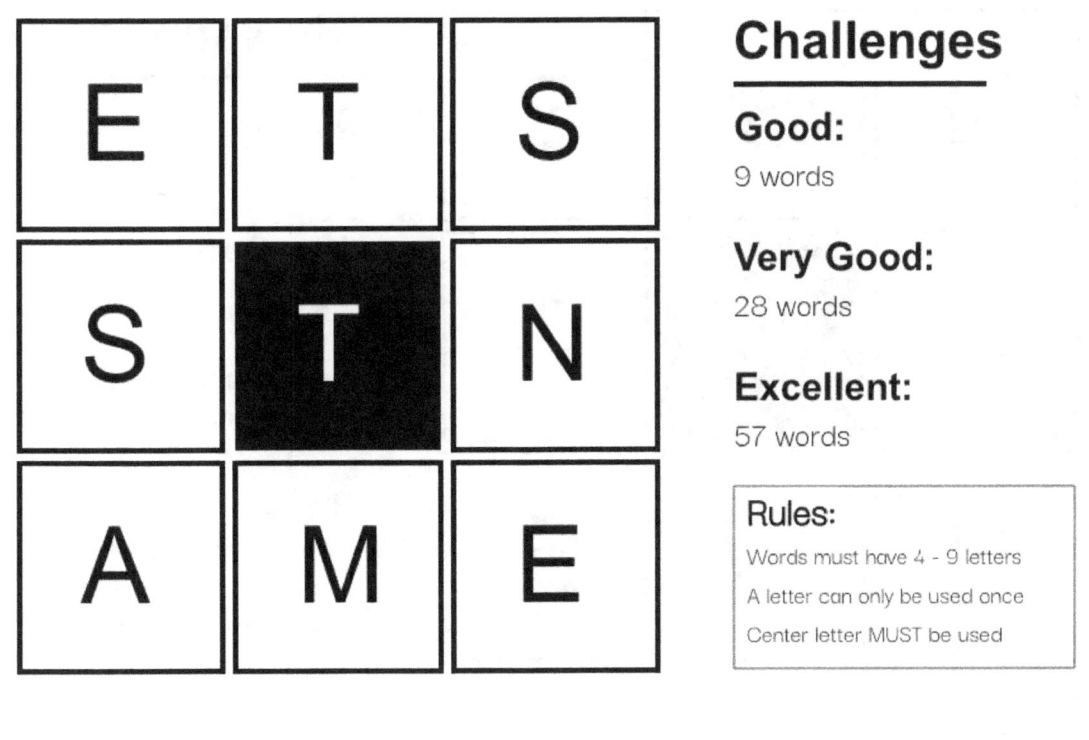

Challenges

Good:
9 words

Very Good:
28 words

Excellent:
57 words

Rules:
Words must have 4 - 9 letters
A letter can only be used once
Center letter MUST be used

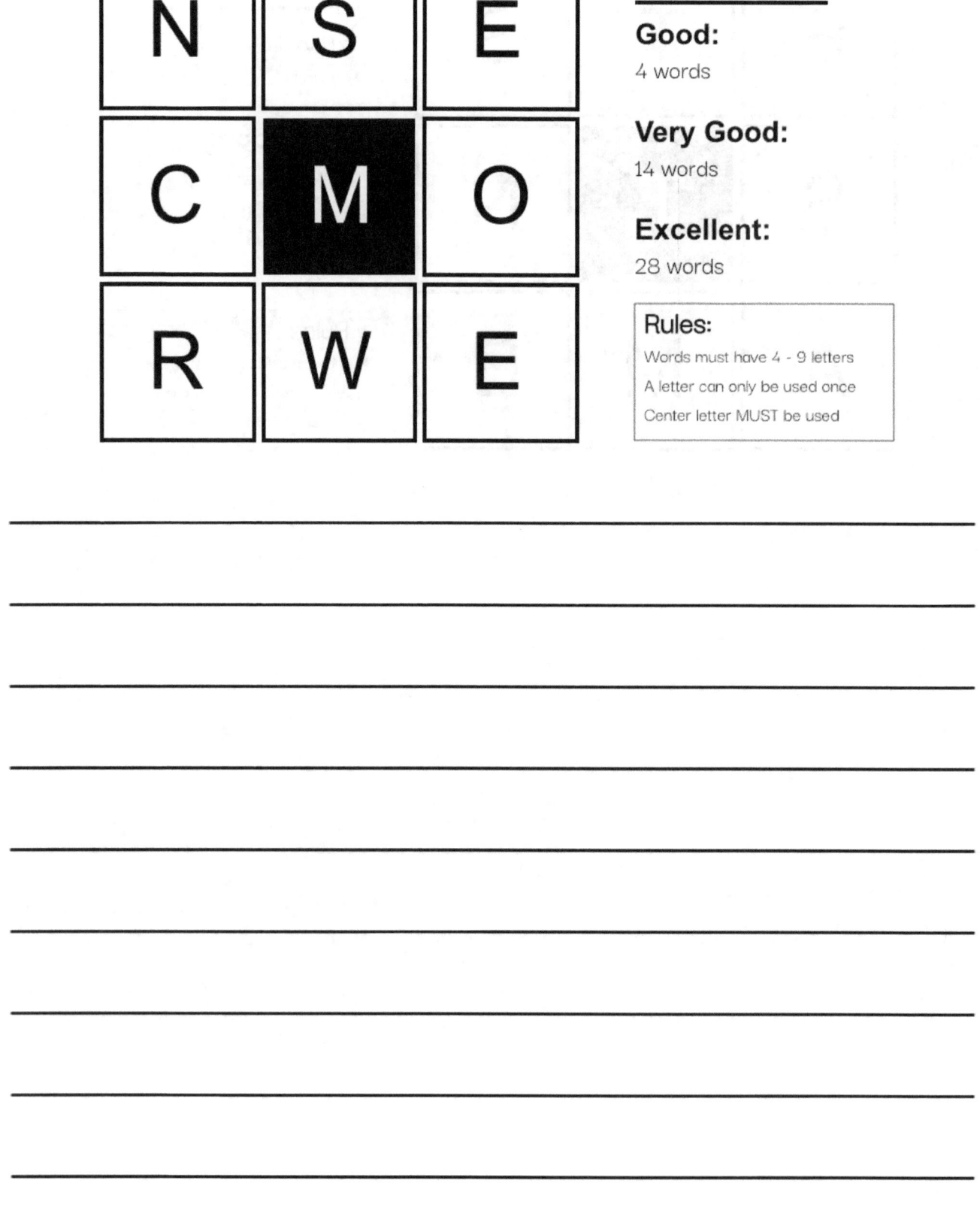

Challenges

Good:
5 words

Very Good:
15 words

Excellent:
30 words

Rules:
Words must have 4 - 9 letters
A letter can only be used once
Center letter MUST be used

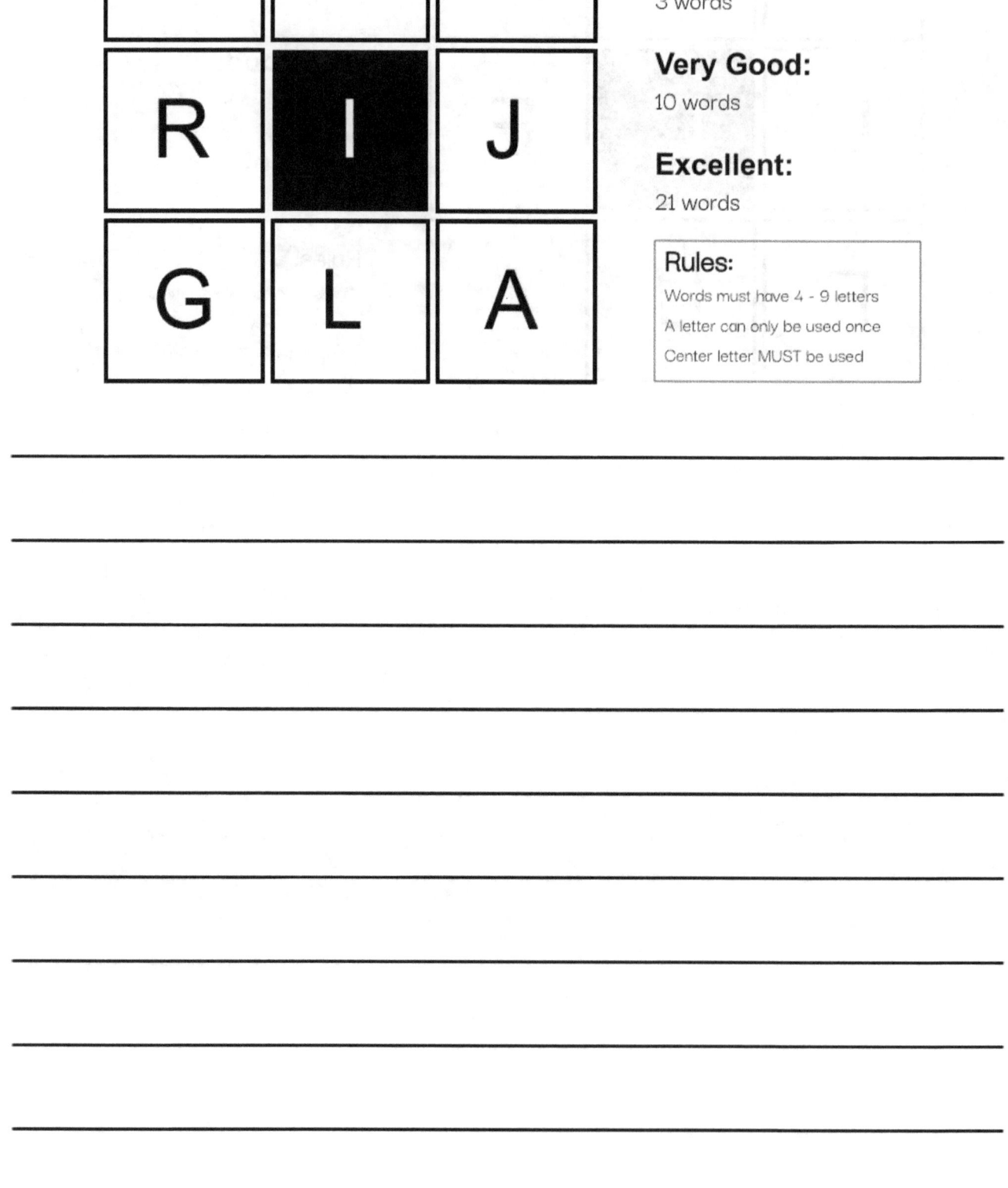

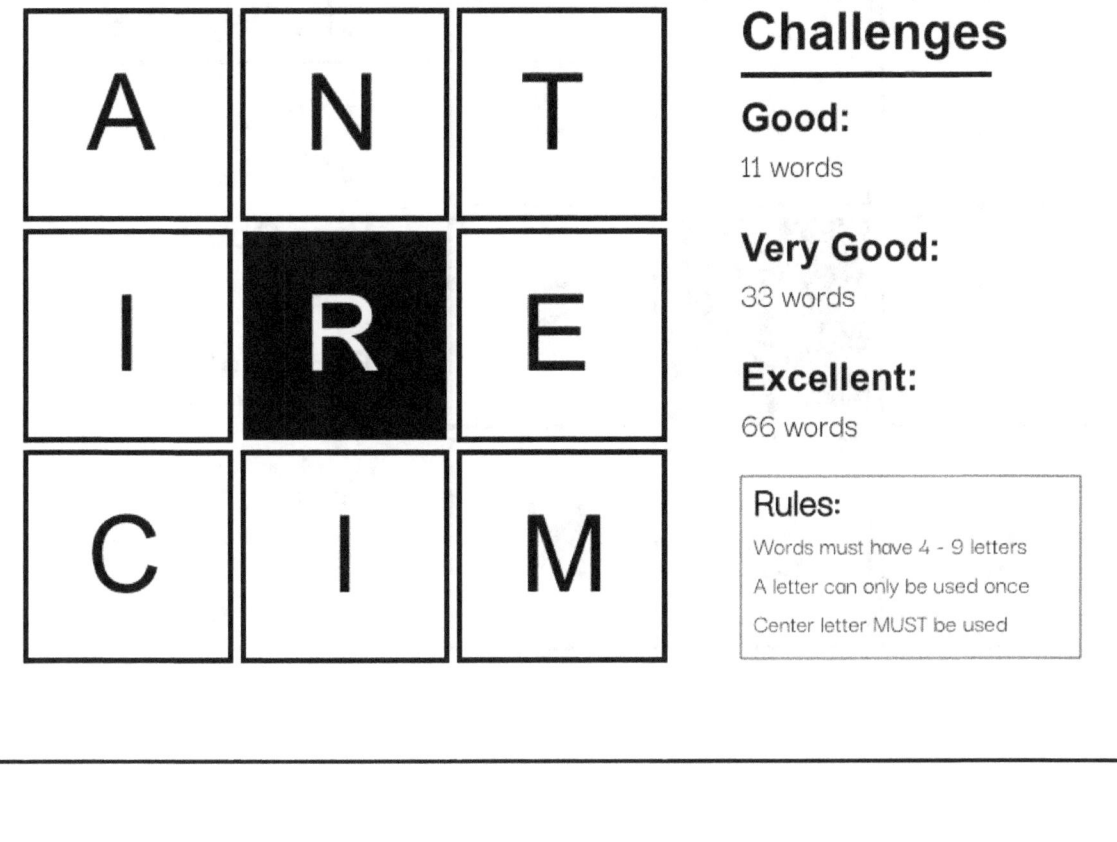

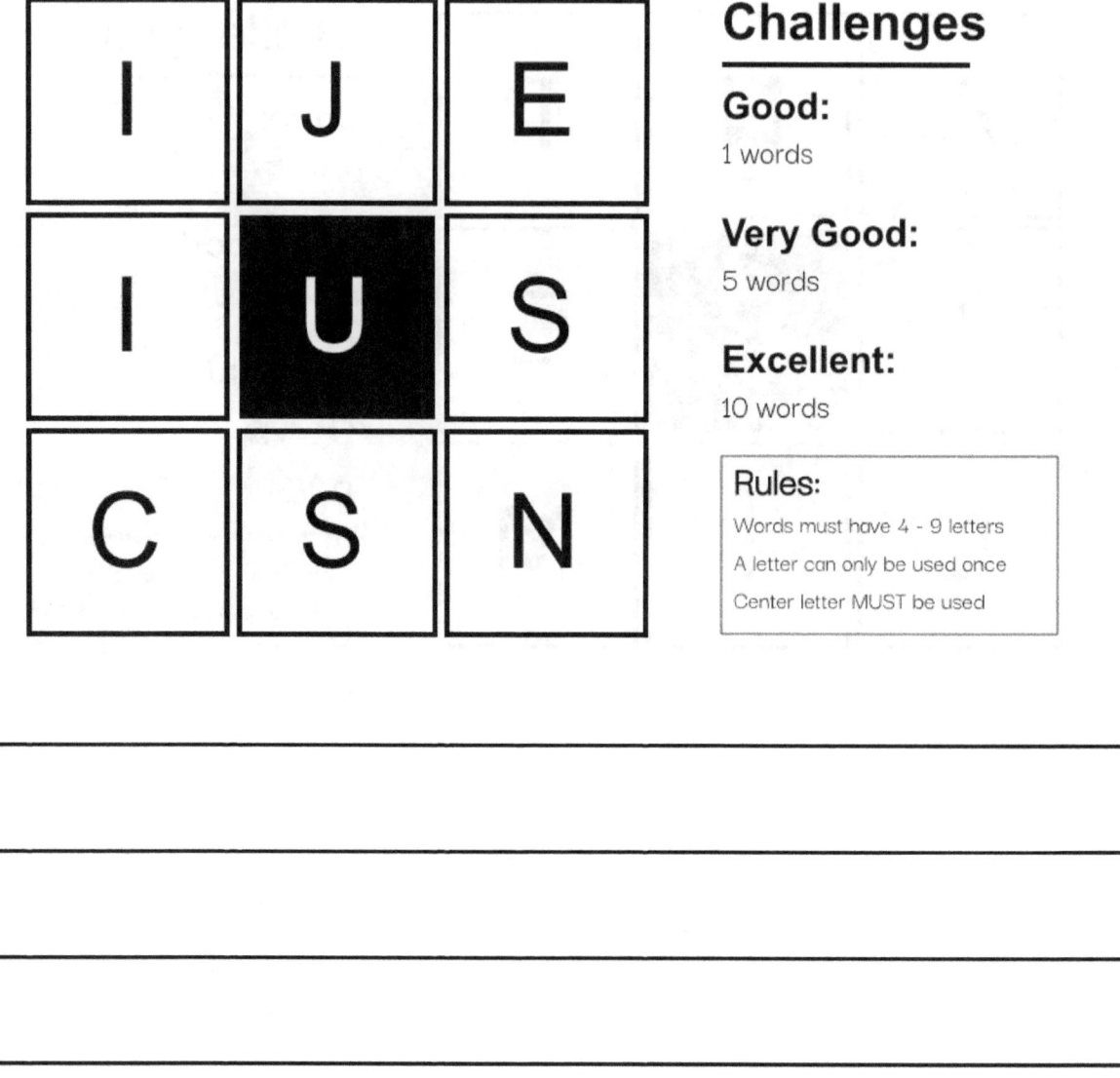

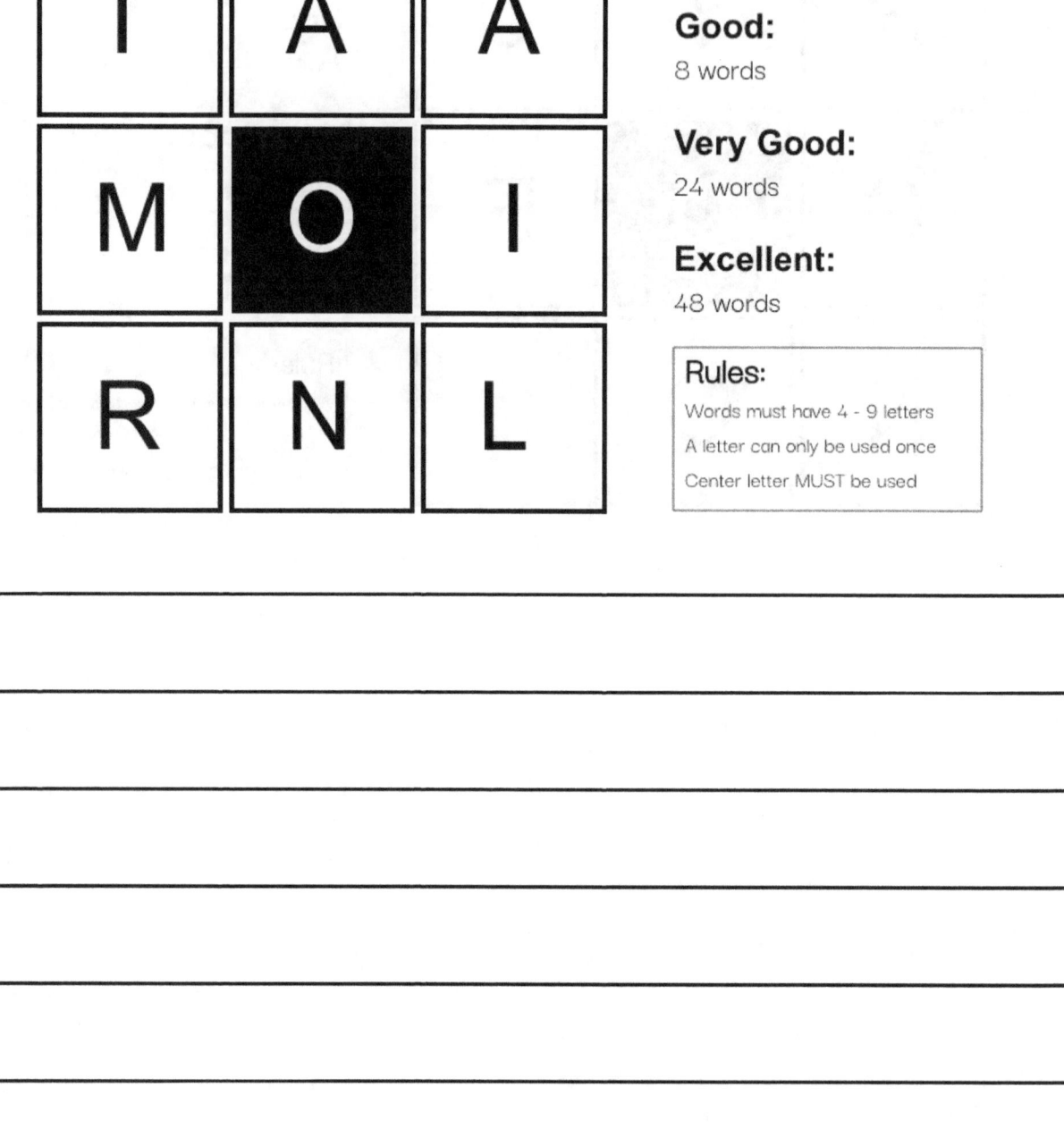

100

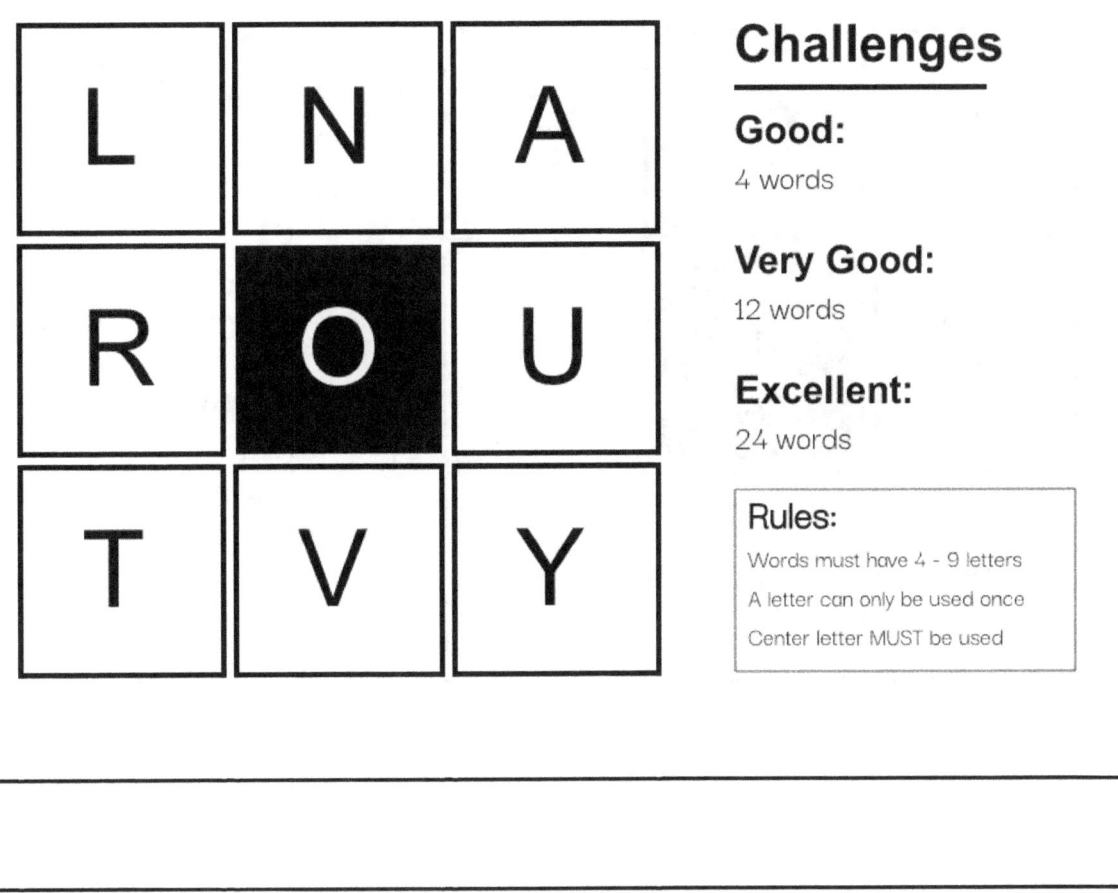

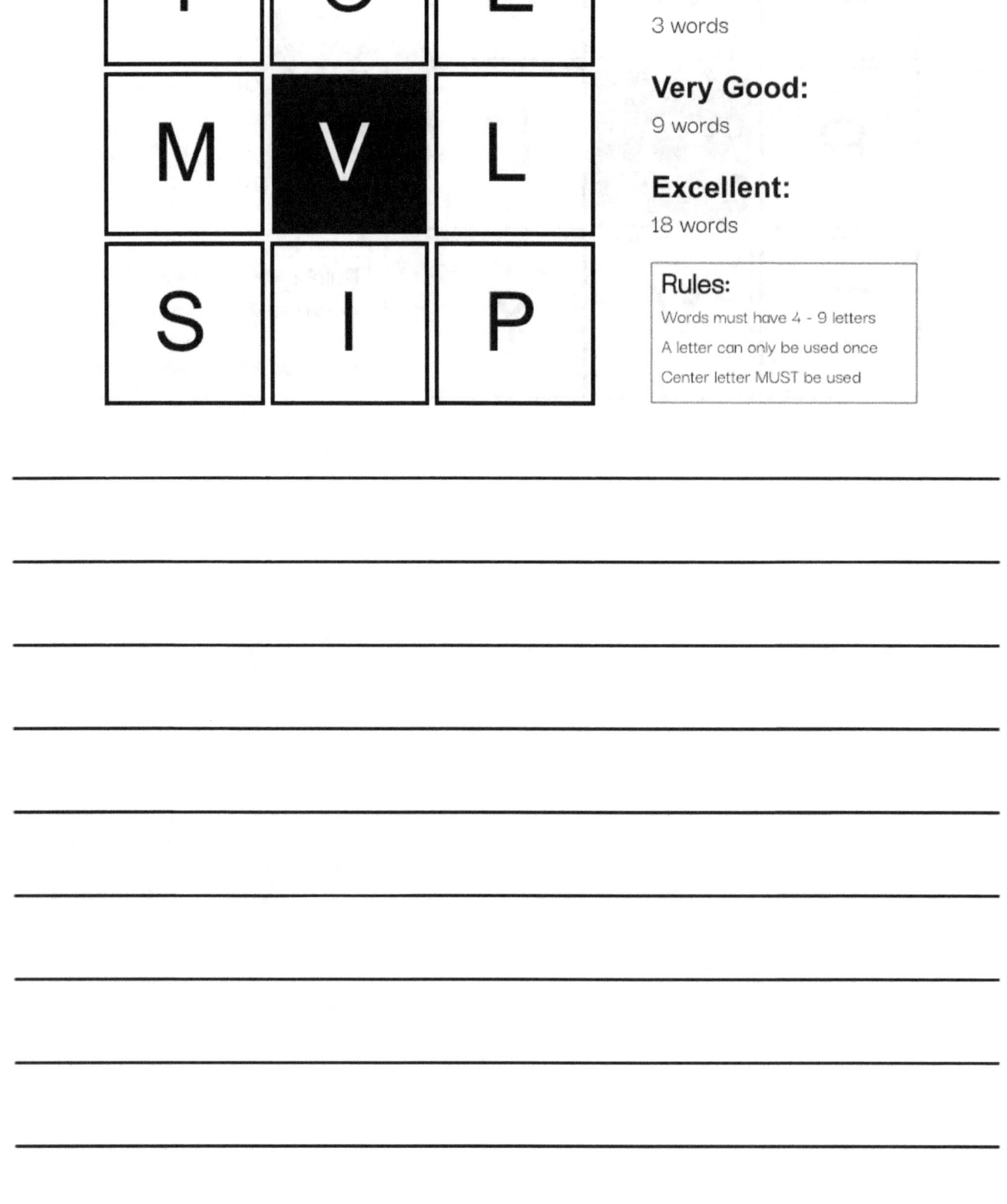

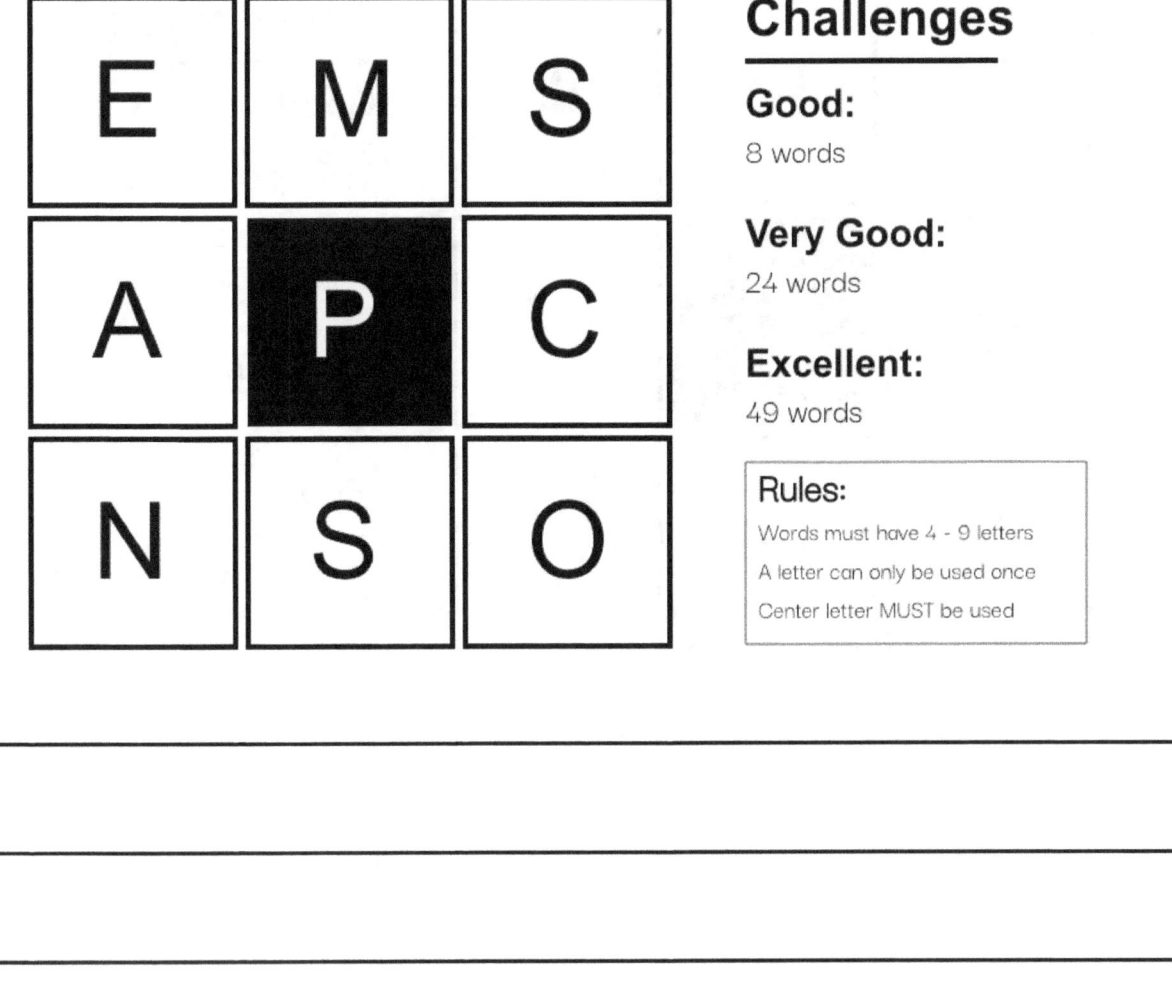

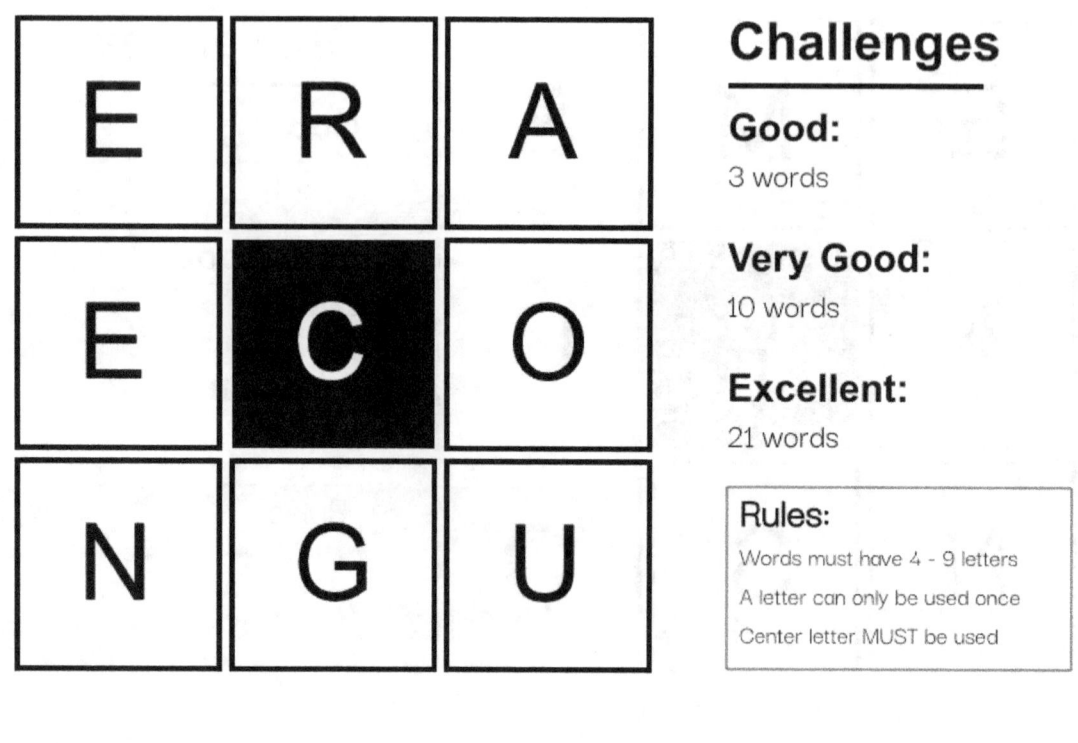

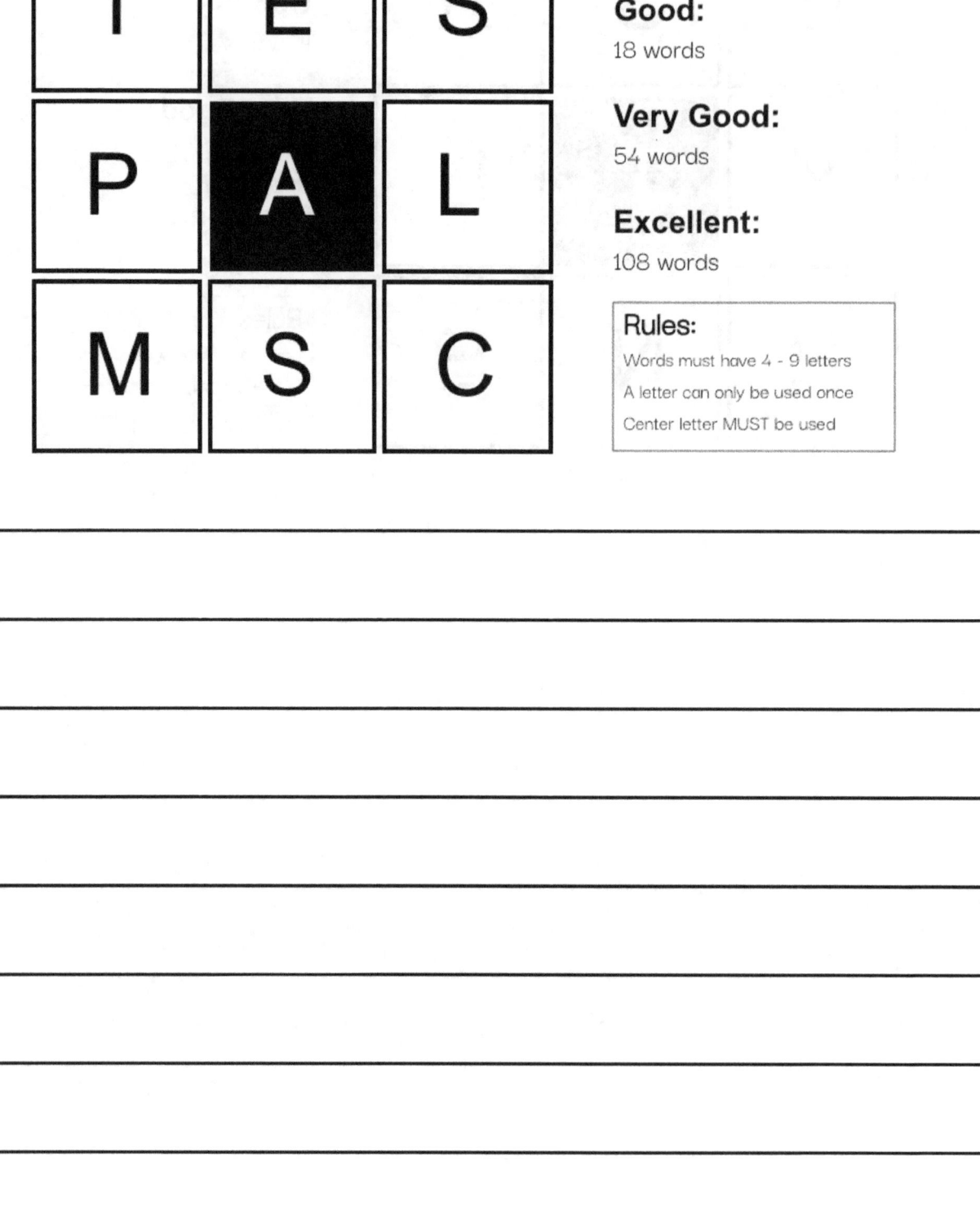

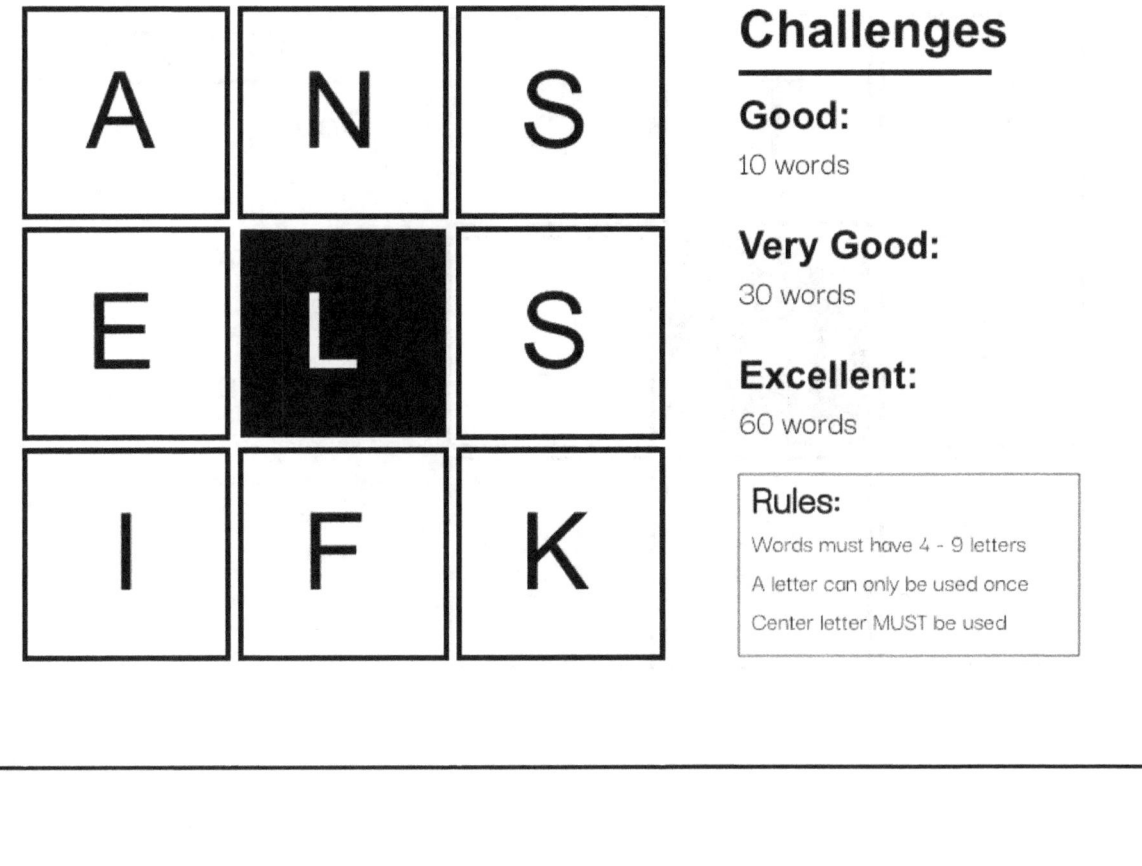

Challenges

Good:
10 words

Very Good:
30 words

Excellent:
60 words

Rules:
Words must have 4 - 9 letters
A letter can only be used once
Center letter MUST be used

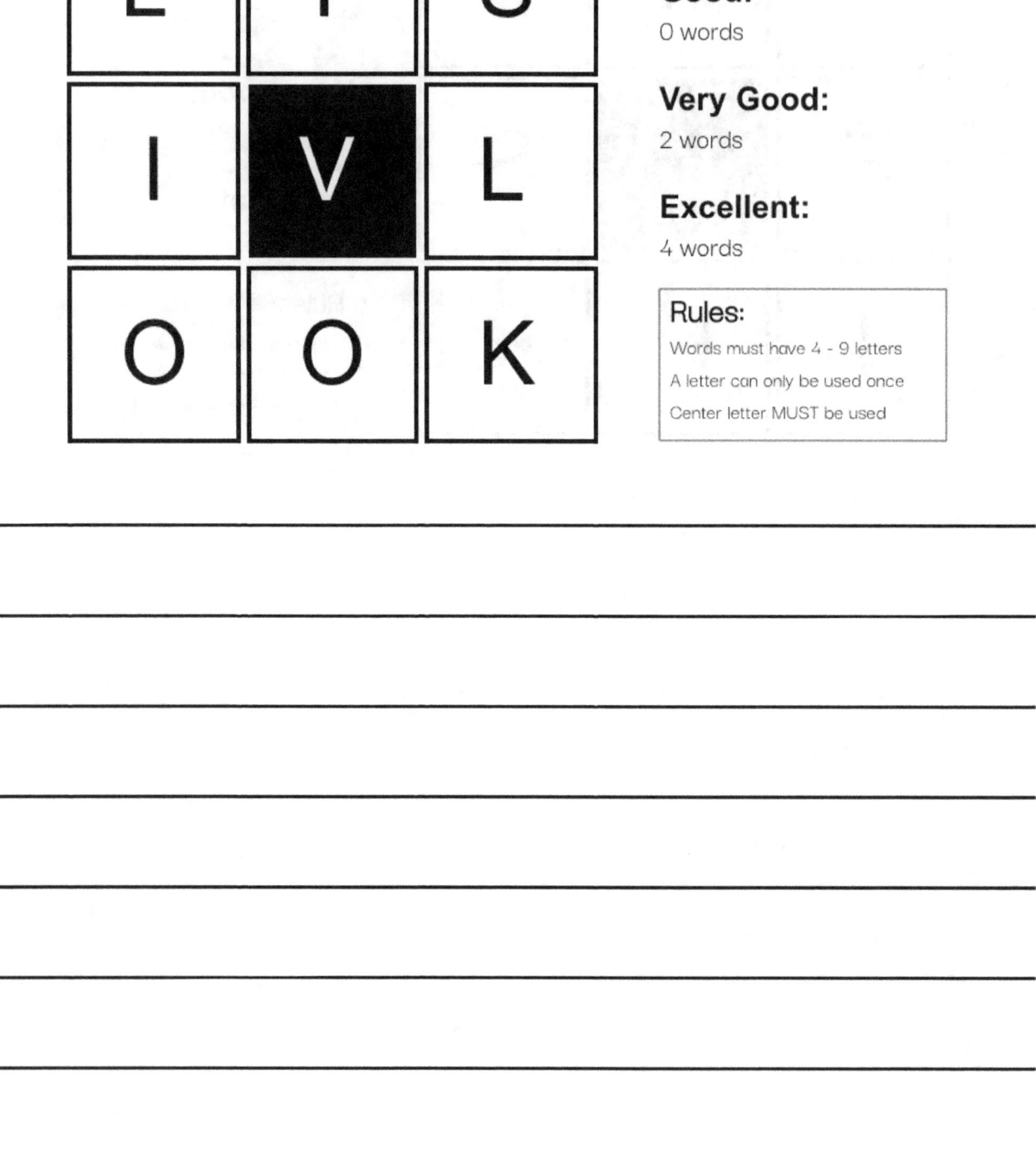

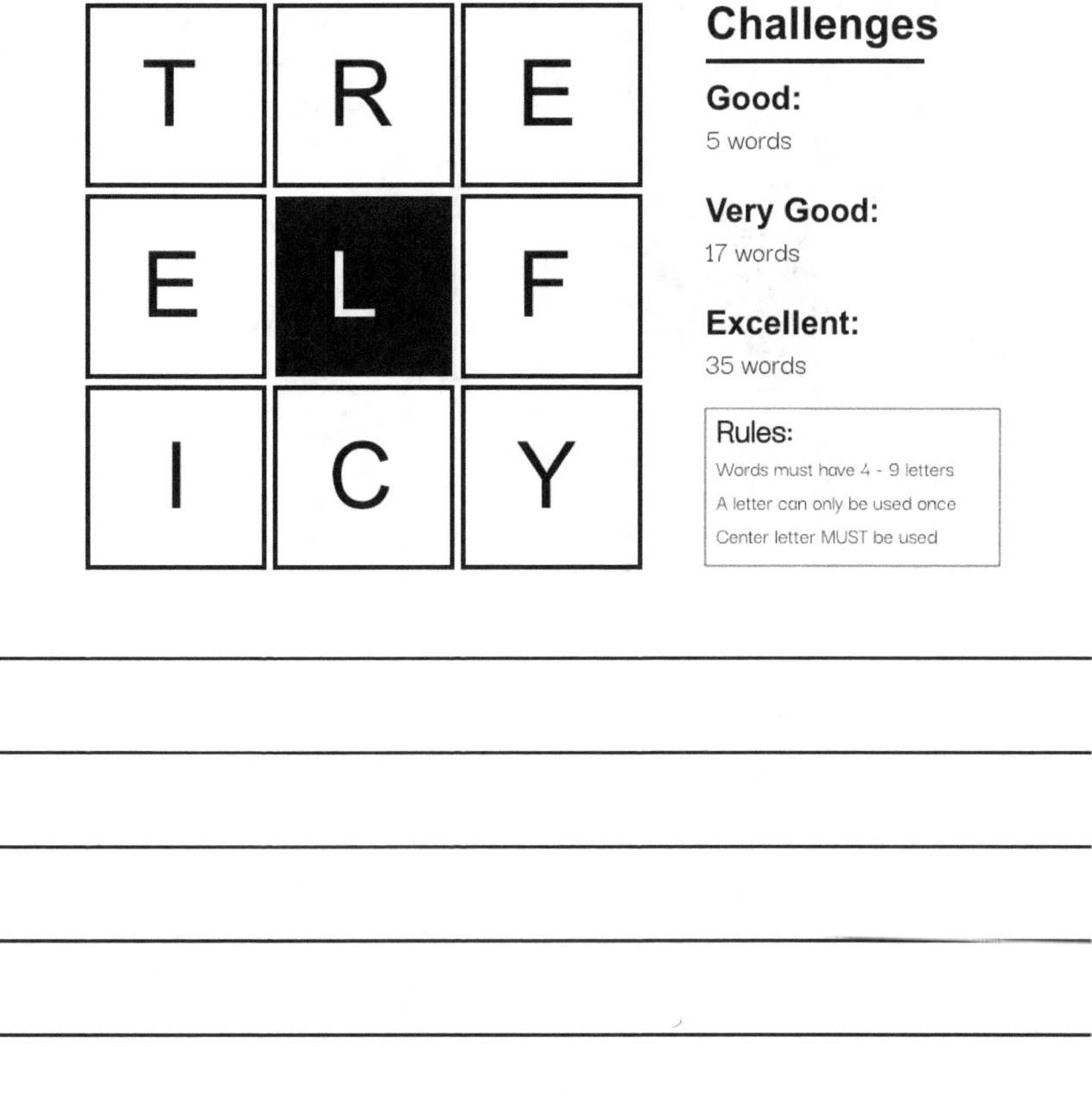

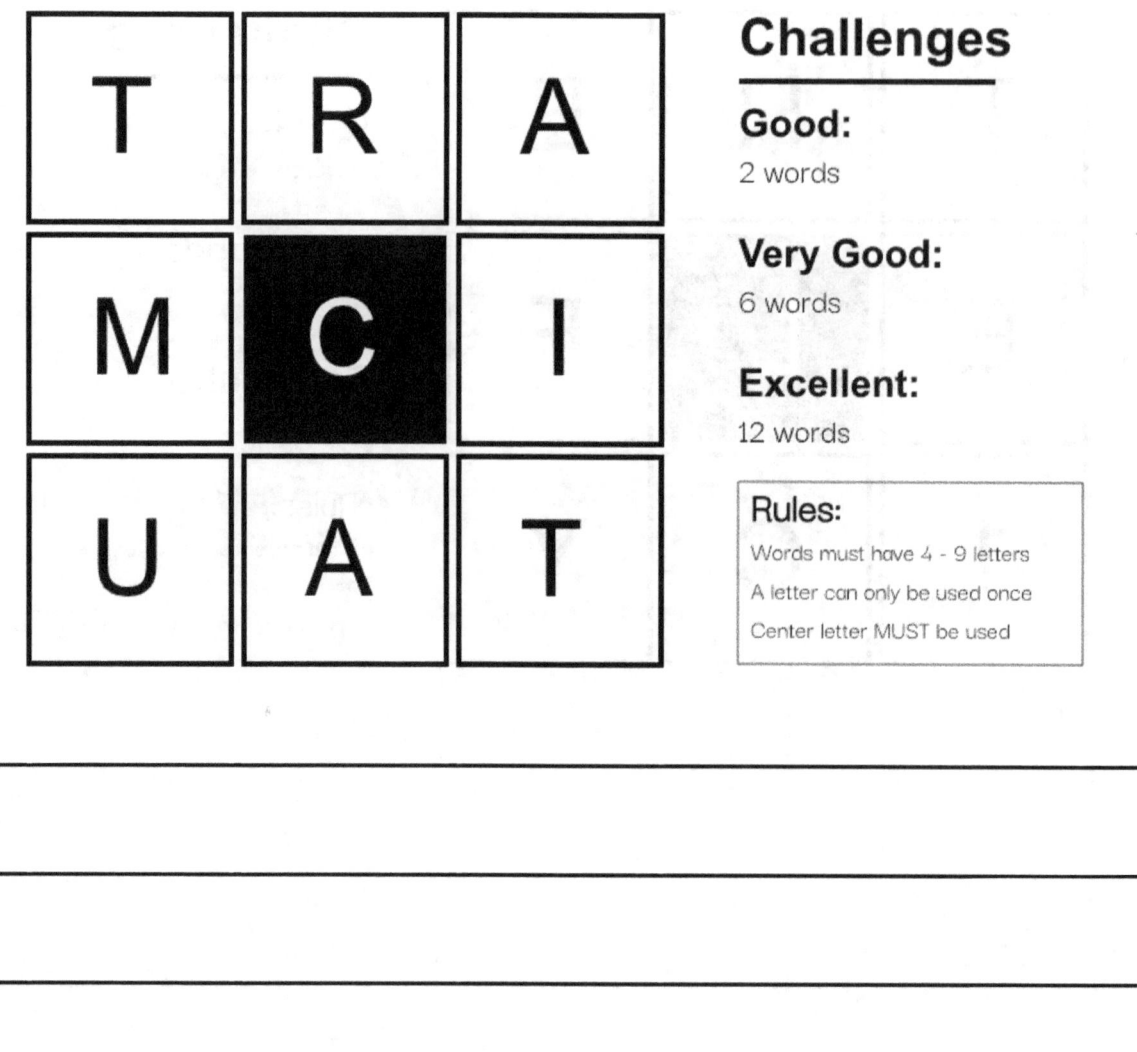

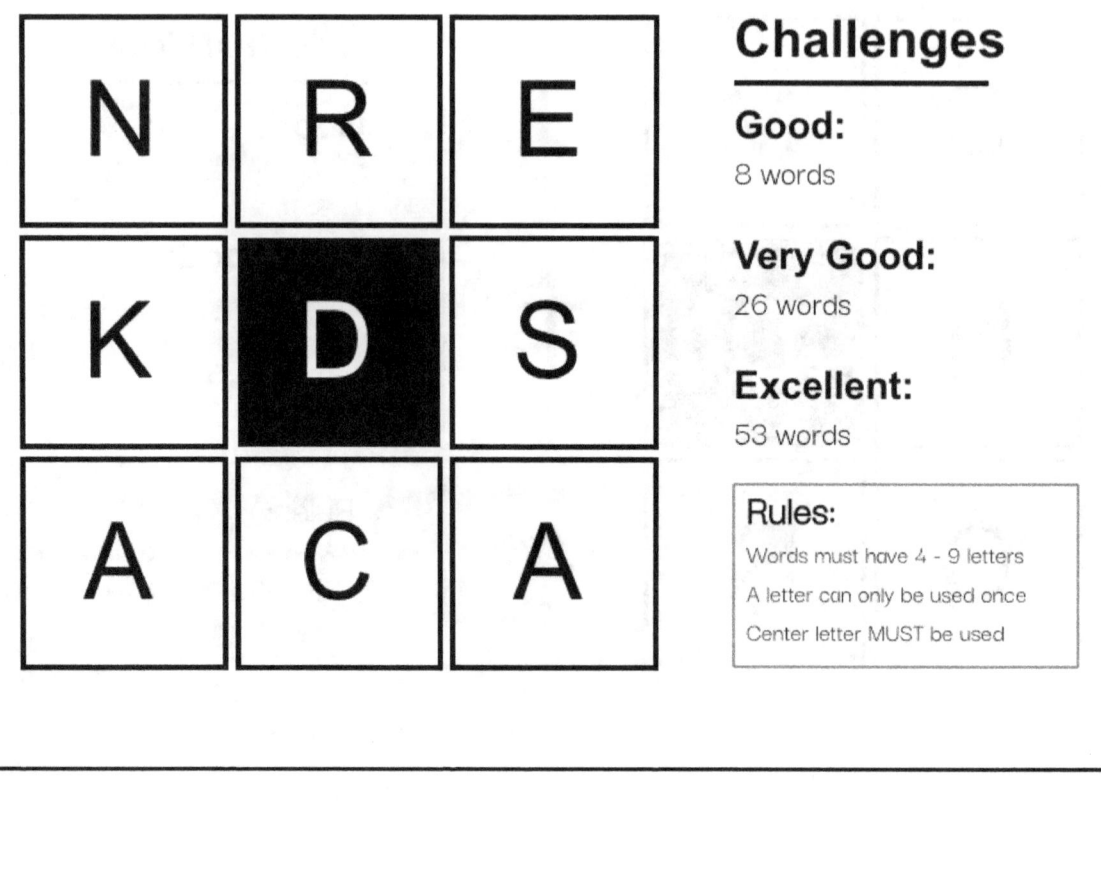

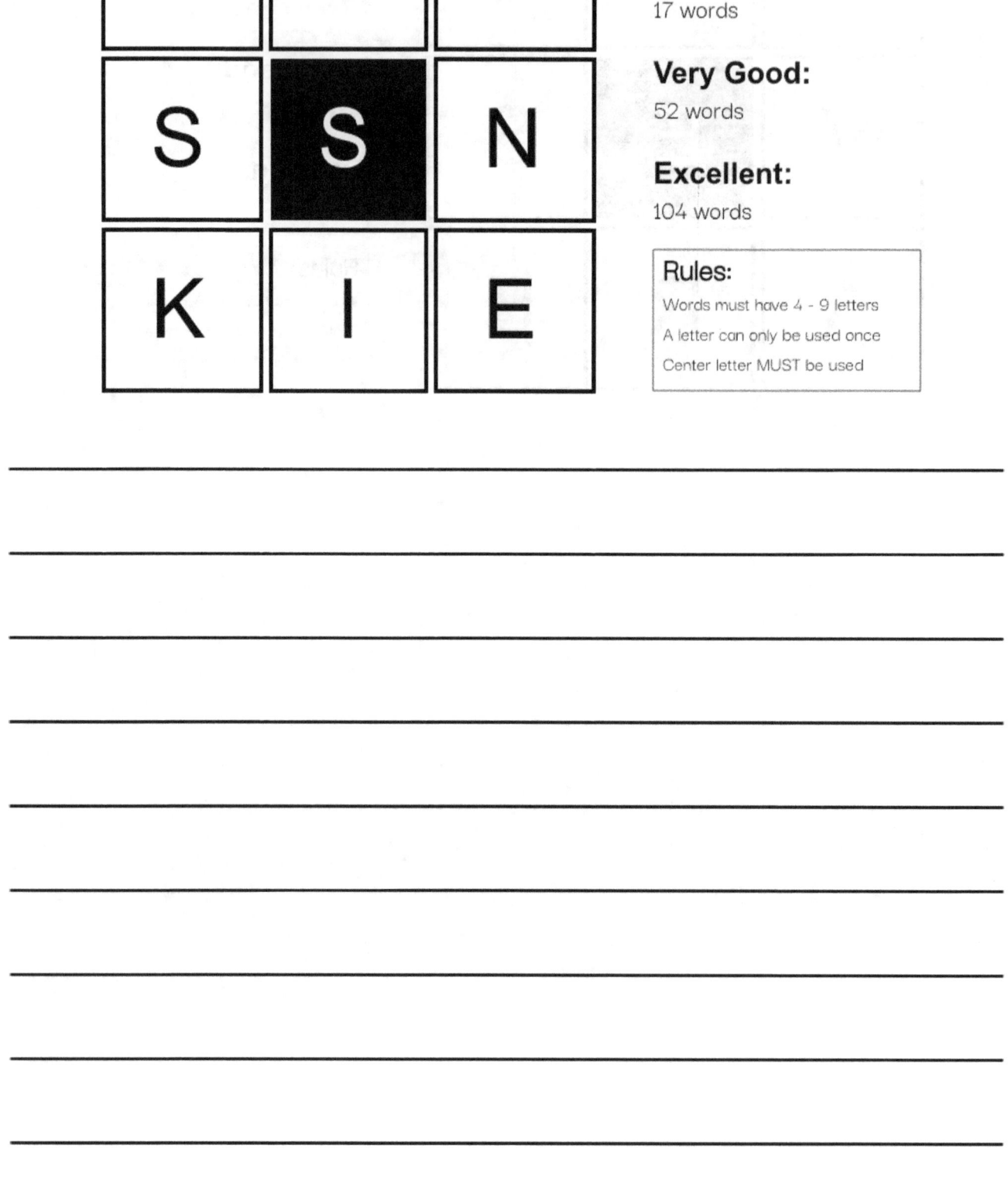

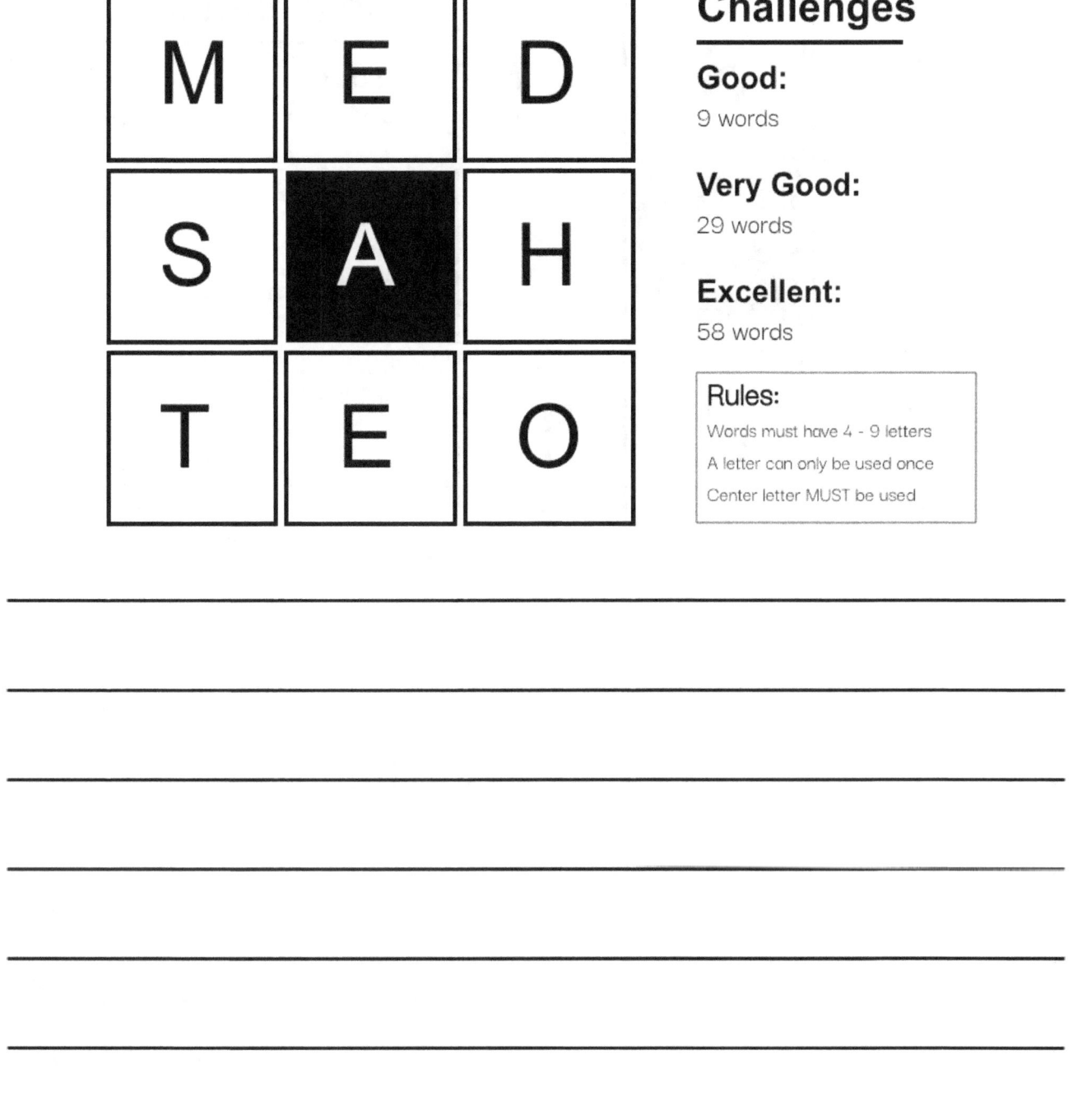

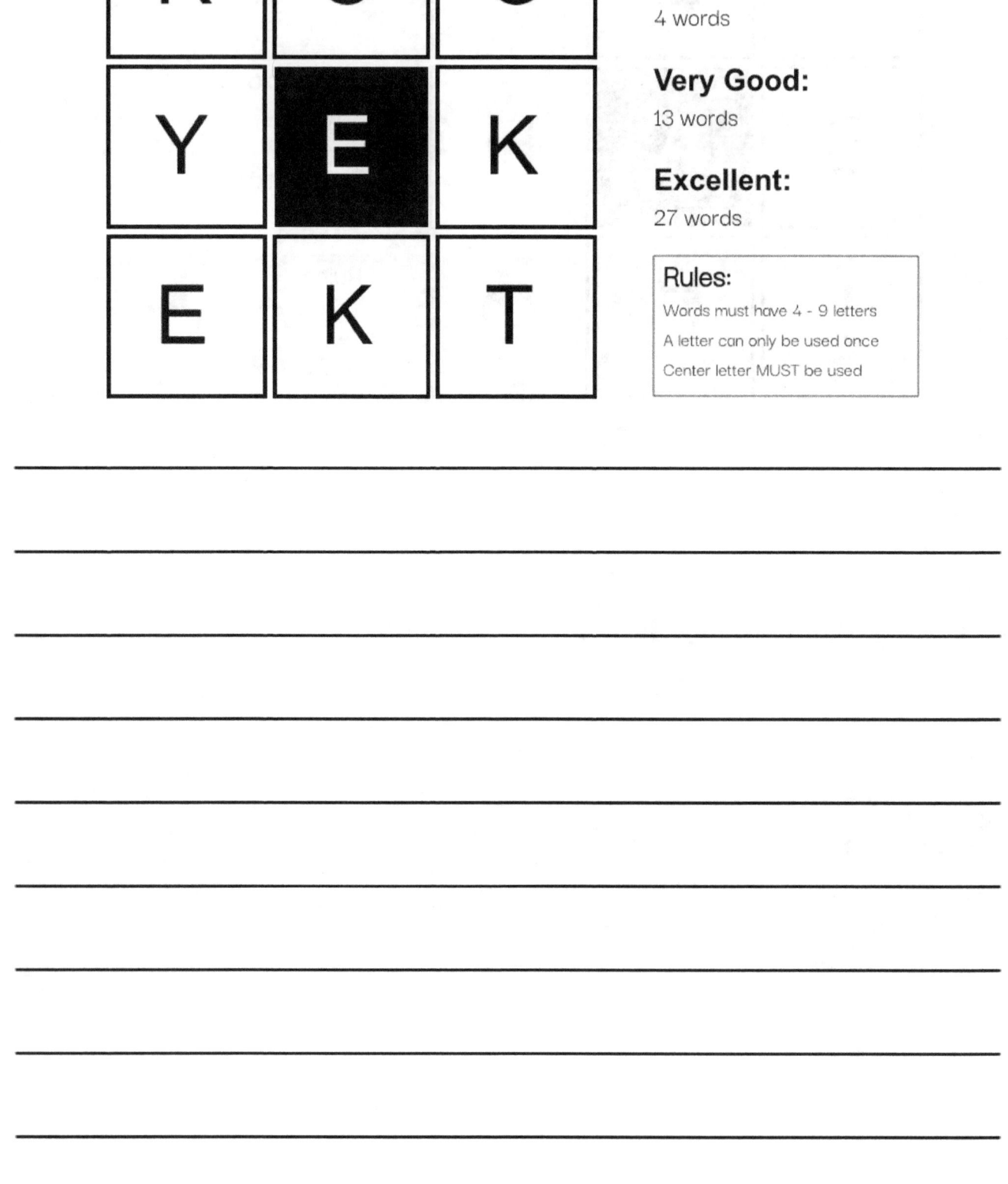

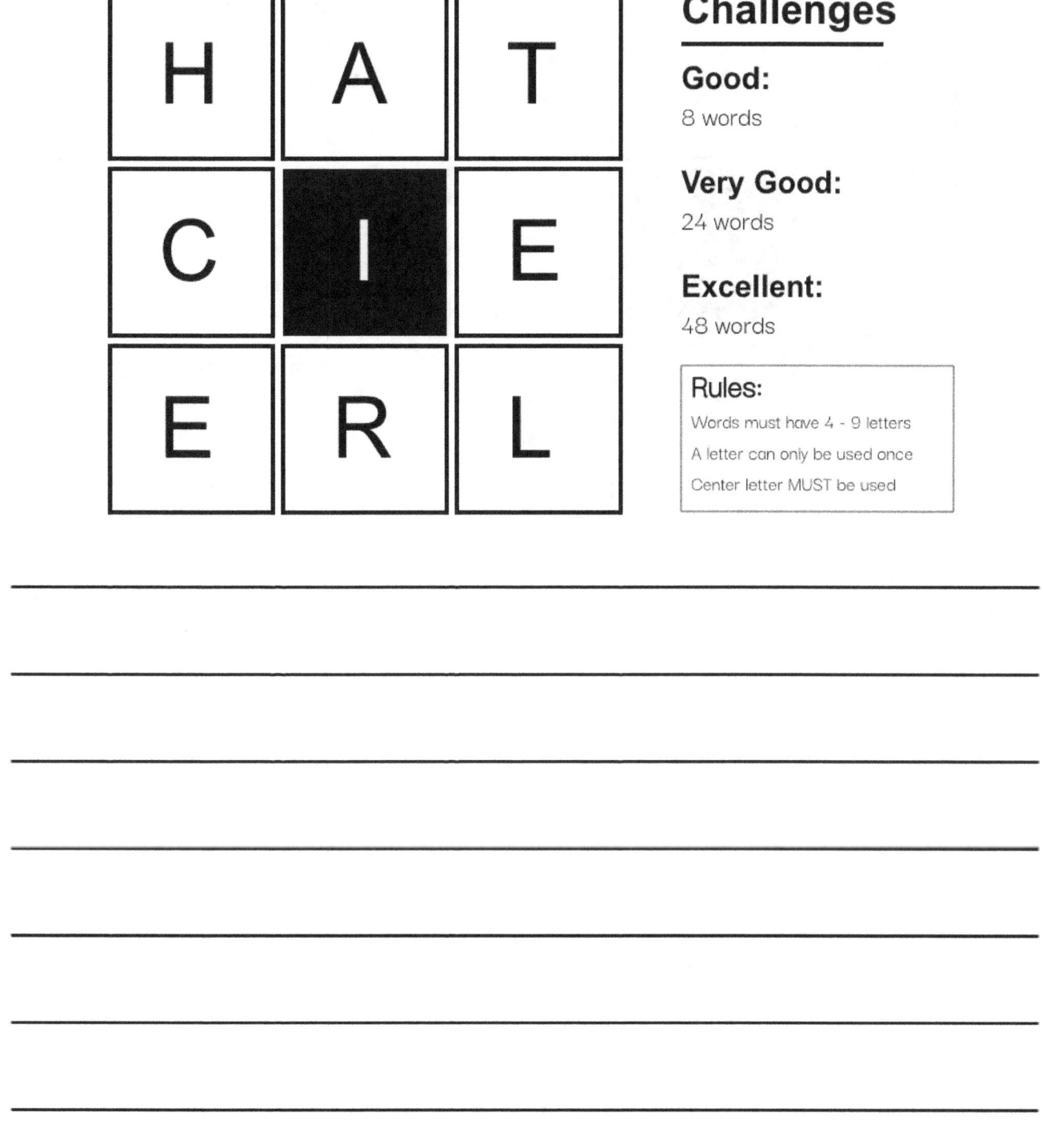

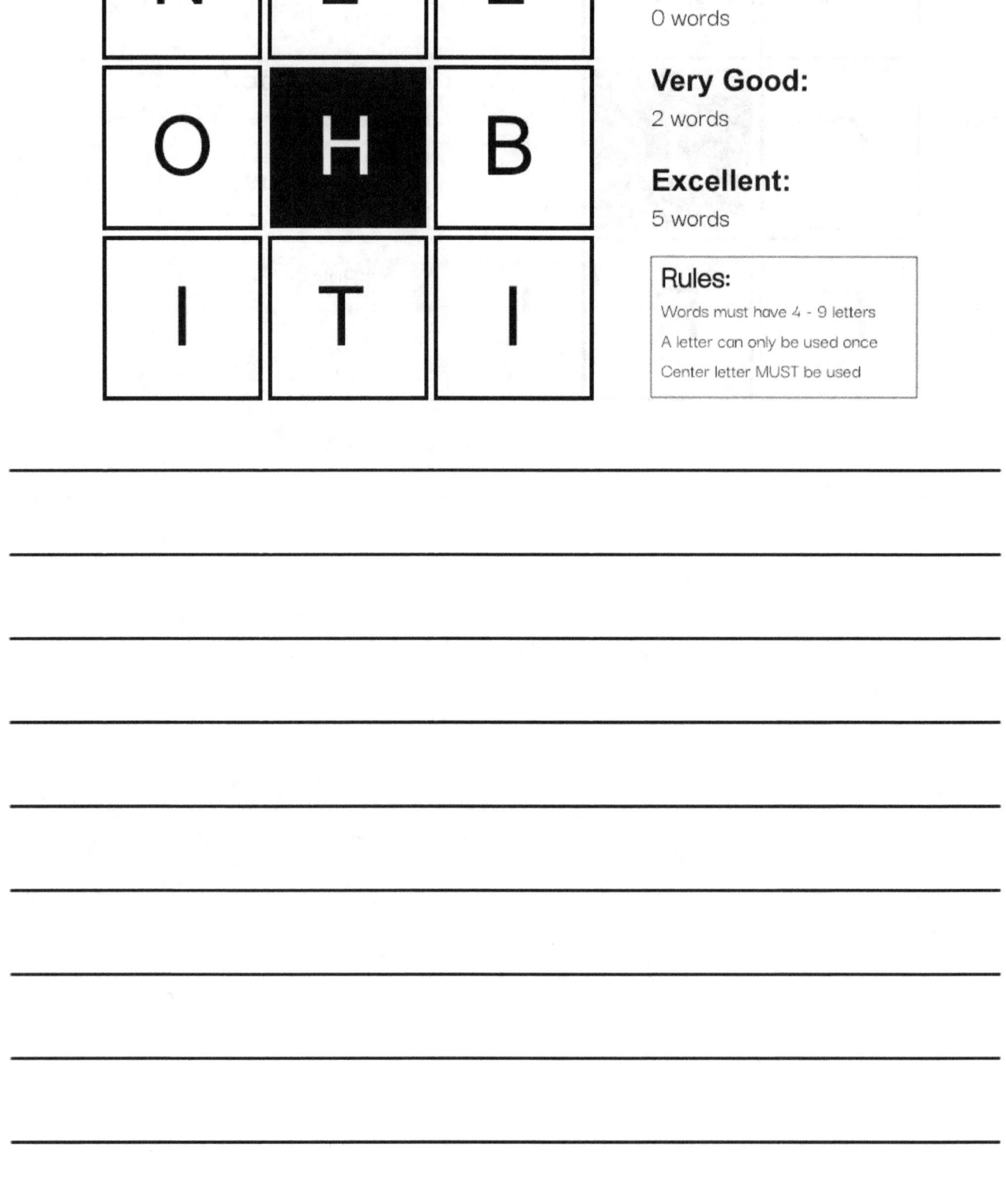

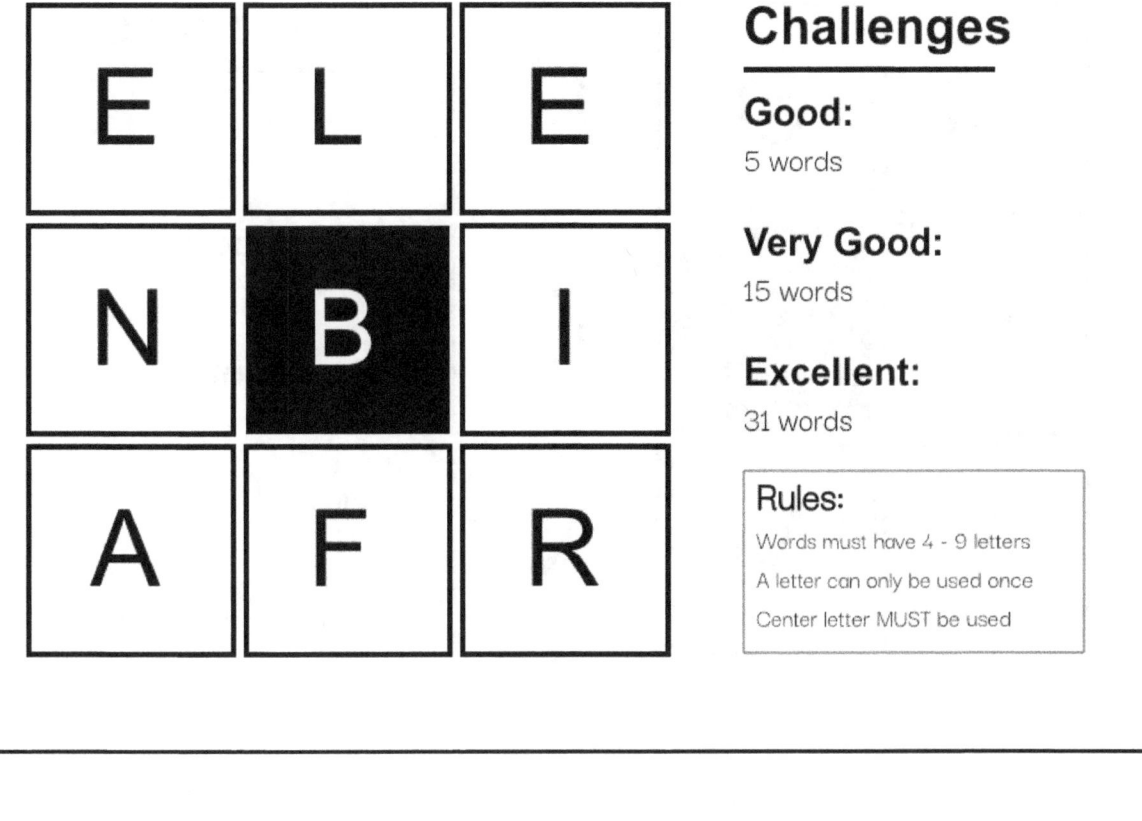

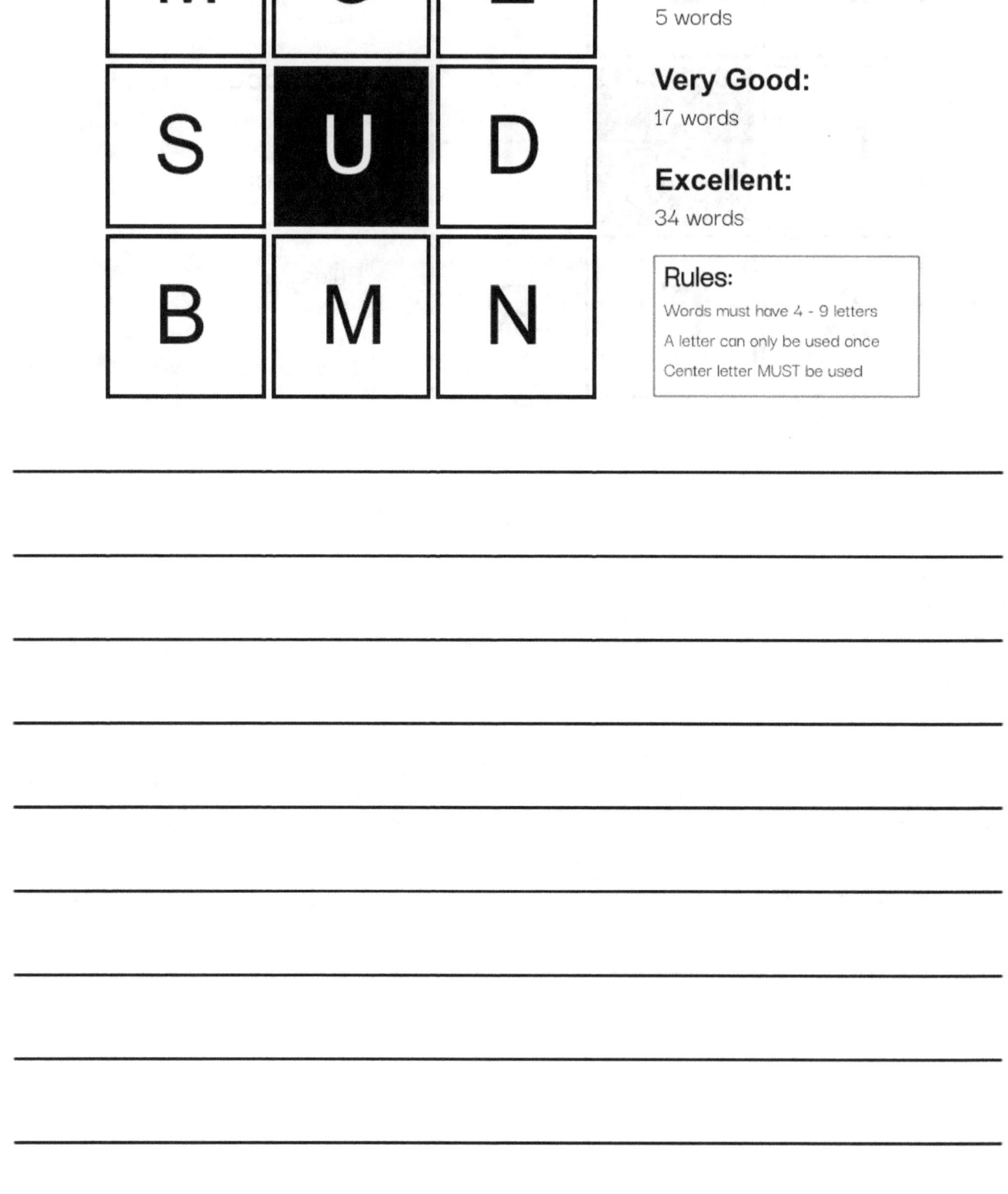

Solutions

1

4 Letter Words — Words: 38

adam, aped, dame, damp, data, date, edam, made, mate, mead, meat, pate, peat, puma, tame, tamp, tape, taut, team, teat, tuta

5 Letter Words

adapt, adept, datum, mated, matte, tamed, tampa, taped, taupe

6 Letter Words

matted, mutate, patted, tamped, update

7 Letter Words

mutated

8 Letter Words

amputate

9 Letter Words

amputated

2

4 Letter Words — Words: 39

core, corn, cory, ergo, gore, gory, gyre, gyro, lore, lyre, nero, ogre, orgy, oyer, rely, reno, role, yore

5 Letter Words

ceorl, color, corey, corny, coyer, crone, crony, croon, glory, goner, loner, negro, royce

6 Letter Words

clergy, conger, cooler, longer, oleron, oregon

7 Letter Words

cryogen

8 Letter Words

9 Letter Words

necrology

3

4 Letter Words — Words: 74

airs, ansi, bias, bier, bins, brie, erin, iran, iras, isbn, nazi, nibs, rain, rein, ribs, rien, rise, ruin, sari, seri, sine, sire, size, zuni

5 Letter Words

aires, anise, aries, arise, baize, basin, biens, biers, brain, brian, brine, bruin, burin, ibsen, inure, nazis, rains, raise, reins, rinse, risen, ruins, siren, urine, zaire, zunis

6 Letter Words

airbus, arisen, arsine, brains, braise, brines, bruise, brunei, buries, burins, busier, insure, inures, rabies, rubies, serbia, ursine, zanies, zanier

7 Letter Words

serbian

8 Letter Words

suzerain, urbanize

9 Letter Words

urbanizes

4

4 Letter Words — Words: 157

airs, ansi, anti, erin, iran, iras, nits, rain, rein, rien, rise, rite, sari, seri, sine, sins, sire, sirs, site, sits, snit, stir, tier, ties, tina, tine, tins, tint, tire, tits

5 Letter Words

aires, anise, antis, aries, arise, artis, astir, entia, inert, inset, inter, intra, irate, rains, raise, reins, reits, resin, resit, rinse, risen, rises, rites, saint, saris, satin, siren, sires, sitae, sitar, sites, snits, stain, stair, stein, sties, stint, stirs, taint, tarsi, tiers, tines, tints, tires, titan, train, trait, tries, trine, trite

6 Letter Words

anises, arisen, arises, arsine, artist, attire, insert, insets, instar, inters, raises, ratite, resins, resist, resits, retain, retina, rinses, saints, sansei, satins, satire, siesta, sinter, sirens, sister, sitars, sitter, stains, stairs, steins, stints, strain, strait, taints, testis, tisane, titans, trains, traits, trines

7 Letter Words

artiest, artiste, artists, attires, inserts, instate, nastier, nattier, nitrate, ratites, resiant, retains, retinas, retsina, satinet, satires, sestina, sinters, sitters, strains, straits, striate, tansies, tastier, tertian, tisanes, transit

8 Letter Words

artistes, instates, nastiest, nitrates, satinets, straiten, transits

9 Letter Words

resistant, straitens

Solutions

5

4 Letter Words

anew	awes	ewer	ewes	news	sawn	saws	sewn	sews
swan	wane	ware	warn	wars	wean	wear	weir	wens
were	wine	wins	wire	wise	wren			

5 Letter Words

ewers	newer	renew	sewer	sinew	swain	swans
swear	swine	wanes	wares	warns	weans	wears
weirs	wines	wires	wiser	wises	wrens	

6 Letter Words

answer	renews	seesaw	sewers	sinews	swains
swears	wiener				

7 Letter Words

answers	newsier	wearies	wieners

8 Letter Words

wariness

9 Letter Words

weariness

6

Words: 79

4 Letter Words

bare	barn	bart	bear	bern	bert	brae	bran	brat
brut	burn	burr	burt	earn	hare	hart	hear	herb
hurt	narr	near	rant	rare	rate	rear	rent	rhea
ruat	rube	rune	runt	ruth	tare	tear	tern	turn
urea								

5 Letter Words

autre	barer	berth	brunt	brute	burnt	earth
hater	heart	nehru	rebut	reran	rerun	terra
truer	tuber	tuner	unbar	urban		

6 Letter Words

anther	arthur	banter	barren	barter	bather
bertha	breath	brunet	bunter	burner	errant
hunter	nature	rather	return	tehran	turban
turner	urbane				

7 Letter Words

unearth   urethra

8 Letter Words

9 Letter Words

heartburn

7

Words: 18

4 Letter Words

foot	goth	gout	hoot	thug	tofu	togo	toot
toto	tout	tuft	tutu				

5 Letter Words

ought   outgo   tooth   tough

6 Letter Words

fought

7 Letter Words

8 Letter Words

9 Letter Words

outfought

8

Words: 110

4 Letter Words

deer	doer	dorm	eros	herd	here	hero	hers	hors	mere
mers	more	mors	mort	ores	redo	reds	reed	rest	rode
rods	roes	rome	rose	rosh	rote	rots	seer	sere	sore
sort	term	tore	tree	trod					

5 Letter Words

deter	doers	dorms	erode	ester	ether	herds	heres
homer	horde	horse	meter	metro	mores	morse	other
reeds	reset	rhode	rotes	seder	sheer	shore	short
shred	steer	store	storm	terms	terse	there	three
throe	treed	trees					

6 Letter Words

dehors	desert	deters	erodes	ethers	hereto	hermes
heroes	homers	hordes	horsed	merest	meteor	meters
metros	mother	others	redoes	remote	rested	rhodes
shored	sorted	stereo	stored	strode	termed	termes
threes	throes					

7 Letter Words

meteors	mothers	shorted	smother	stormed	theorem
thermos					

8 Letter Words

mothered   theorems

9 Letter Words

smothered

Solutions

9

4 Letter Words — Words: 91

acts	ails	alit	also	alto	alts	cast	cats	coal
coat	cola	iota	ital	laic	laos	lass	last	lisa
loca	oats	ocas	oval	sacs	sail	salt	scat	slat
slav	sola	taco	tail	talc	vast	vats	vial	visa
vita								

5 Letter Words

altos	ascot	casts	cavil	cista	class	coals		
coast	coati	coats	colas	costa	lasso	lasts		
oasis	octal	ovals	sails	salic	salts	salvo		
scats	sisal	slats	slavs	tacos	tails	vatic		
vials	viola	visas	vista	vital	vitas	vocal		
volta								

6 Letter Words

ascots	cavils	coasts	coatis	coital	salvos
scotia	slavic	social	violas	vistas	vitals
vocals					

7 Letter Words

socials   stoical   voltaic

8 Letter Words

vocalist

9 Letter Words

vocalists

10

4 Letter Words — Words: 72

leap	nape	neap	pail	pain	pale	pane	pant	pate
peal	peat	pelt	pent	pile	pine	pint	pitt	pity
plan	plat	play	plea	tape	type	yelp		

5 Letter Words

aptly	inapt	inept	leapt	nepal	paint	panel
panty	paten	patty	peaty	penal	petal	petit
petty	pieta	piety	pitta	plain	plait	plane
plant	plate	platt	platy	pleat	plena	

6 Letter Words

alpine	nepali	patent	pilate	pineal	plaint
planet	platen	platte	plenty	pliant	

7 Letter Words

aplenty   ineptly   patient   penalty   pettily
ptyalin   tintype

8 Letter Words

patently

9 Letter Words

patiently

11

4 Letter Words — Words: 34

hint	hone	into	note	open	penh	pent	peon
pine	pint	pony	then	thin	tine	tiny	tone
tony	zion	zone					

5 Letter Words

heinz	honey	inept	opine	peony	phone
phony	pinto	piton	point	ponit	

6 Letter Words

pointy   python   zenith

7 Letter Words

8 Letter Words

9 Letter Words

hypnotize

12

4 Letter Words — Words: 111

cere	deer	dire	drip	eire	eric	erie	heir	herd	here
hers	hire	peer	pere	pier	pres	pris	reds	reed	reps
rice	rich	ride	rids	ripe	rips	rise	seer	sere	seri
sire									

5 Letter Words

cheer	chirp	chris	cider	creed	creep	crepe	cried
cries	crisp	dicer	dries	drips	eider	heirs	herds
heres	hired	hires	peers	perch	piers	prece	price
pride	pried	pries	reeds	reich	riche	rides	scire
scrip	seder	sheer	shier	shire	shred	sired	spire
spree							

6 Letter Words

cerise	cheers	chirps	ciders	cipher	creeds	creeps
crepes	desire	dicers	eiders	herpes	perish	pierce
priced	prices	prides	recipe	reship	reside	riches
screed	sphere	spider				

7 Letter Words

chirped	ciphers	crisped	decries	perched	perches
pierced	pierces	precise	preside	recipes	

8 Letter Words

ciphered   decipher   perished

9 Letter Words

deciphers

Solutions

13

4 Letter Words — **Words: 88**

eire, erie, erin, gelt, gene, gent, glee, glen, leer
leet, lege, lent, lien, line, lire, lite, neil, nile
reel, rein, rent, rien, rile, rite, teen, tent, tern
tier, tile, tine, tire, tree

5 Letter Words

egret, eigne, elite, enter, genet, genie, genre
green, greet, inert, inlet, intel, inter, irene
legit, liege, liner, liter, nigel, niger, regni
reign, retie, rette, tenet, tiger, tiler, tinge
title, trine, trite

6 Letter Words

elegit, engirt, entire, gentle, letter, linger
litter, nettle, regent, relent, reline, teeing
teneri, tingle

7 Letter Words

entitle, gentile, gentler, glitter, integer
leering, letting, reeling, ringlet, treeing

8 Letter Words

9 Letter Words

lettering

14

4 Letter Words — **Words: 152**

ager, ages, ears, ease, east, eats, efts, egos, eras, ergo, ergs, eros, fare, fate, fear, feat
fees, feet, fete, foes, fore, free, fret, gate, gear, gees, gets, goes, gore, ogee, ogre, ores
rage, rase, rate, reae, reef, refs, rest, roes, rose, rote, safe, sage, sate, sear, seat, seer
sego, sera, sere, serf, seta, sore, tare, tear, teas, tees, toes, tore, tree

5 Letter Words

afore, after, agers, agree, arose, aster, eager, eater, egret, erase, ergot, ester, fares
fates, fears, feast, feats, ferae, festa, fetes, forge, forte, frees, freta, frets, gates
gears, gofer, gores, gorse, grate, great, greet, ogees, ogres, orate, rages, rates, reefs
resat, reset, rotes, safer, sager, seato, serge, setae, stage, stare, steer, store, tares
tears, tease, terse, trees

6 Letter Words

agrees, easter, eaters, egrets, ergots, faeroe, faster, fester, forage, forest, forges
forget, fortes, foster, freest, gestae, goatee, gofers, grates, grease, greets, orates
softer, stager, stereo, strafe, teaser

7 Letter Words

faeroes, forages, forgets, goatees, roseate, storage

8 Letter Words

9 Letter Words

forestage, fosterage

15

16

Solutions

17

4 Letter Words — **Words: 60**

afro, aloe, awol, faro, felo, floe, flow, foal, foam, fore, form, fowl, from, loaf, loam, loma, lore, malo, mayo, meow, mole, more, oral, oyer, roam, role, rome, wolf, wore, worm, yore, yowl

5 Letter Words

afore, amore, flora, foamy, foray, forma, foyer, loamy, lower, mayor, molar, moral, moray, morel, mower, rowel, royal, wormy

6 Letter Words

femora, florae, flower, formal, loafer, morale

7 Letter Words

femoral, flowery, wolfram

8 Letter Words

9 Letter Words

mayflower

18

4 Letter Words — **Words: 18**

efts, five, site, sive, stet, test, ties, vest, vets, vies, yeti

5 Letter Words

fives, ivies, testy, yetis

6 Letter Words

feisty

7 Letter Words

testify

8 Letter Words

9 Letter Words

festivity

19

4 Letter Words — **Words: 55**

aces, acta, acte, acts, asia, case, cast, cats, cave, east, eats, iata, sate, save, scat, seat, seta, tact, tats, teas, teat, vase, vast, vats, visa, vita

5 Letter Words

actes, attic, caste, caves, cista, isaac, sitae, state, stave, tacit, taste, teats, vatic, vista, vitae, vitas

6 Letter Words

active, attics, caveat, stacie, static, tacite, vacate

7 Letter Words

actives, caveats, satiate, vacates

8 Letter Words

activate

9 Letter Words

activates

20

4 Letter Words — **Words: 60**

coin, cons, icon, inns, into, ions, jinn, join, nits, noun, nunc, nuns, nuts, onus, sinn, snit, snot, stun, tins, tons, tunc, tuns, unit, unto

5 Letter Words

coins, count, icons, joins, joint, junco, junto, nouns, scion, snout, sonic, sunni, tonic, tunic, tunis, union, units

6 Letter Words

counts, cousin, joints, juncos, juntos, justin, nuncio, tocsin, tonics, tucson, tunics, unions, unison

7 Letter Words

nonsuit, nuncios, suction, unction

8 Letter Words

junction

9 Letter Words

junctions

Solutions

21

4 Letter Words — Words: 108

bleu	blue	boer	bole	bore	byes	byre	clue
core	cube	cues	cure	ecru	eros	lobe	lore
lure	lyre	obey	ores	oyer	rely	reus	robe
role	rose	rube	rues	rule	ruse	ryes	serb
slue	sole	sore	sure	ures	user	yore	yule

cole, lose, roes, sloe

5 Letter Words

beryl	bluer	blues	boers	boles	bores	bruce
buyer	byres	ceorl	close	clues	cores	corey
coyer	cruel	cruse	cubes	cures	curse	lobes
loser	louse	lucre	lures	lyres	obeys	oyers
rebus	robes	roles	rouse	royce	rubes	ruble
rules	score	seoul	slyer	sober	rubles	ulcer

6 Letter Words

blouse	boucle	bourse	burley	buyers	ceorls
closer	coleus	corbel	course	cresol	crusoe
rubles	sorely	source	surely	ulcers	

7 Letter Words

burleys, closure, corbels, obscure, soberly

8 Letter Words

9 Letter Words

obscurely

22

4 Letter Words — Words: 32

etym	moor	moot	mope	more	mort	mote	perm
poem	prom	rome	romp	room	temp	term	tome

5 Letter Words

empty	metro	motet	motor	motto	proem
promo	romeo	roomy	tempo	tempt	totem
tromp					

6 Letter Words

emptor

7 Letter Words

promote

8 Letter Words

9 Letter Words

optometry

23

4 Letter Words — Words: 83

ages	ague	east	eats	efts	emit	emus	esau	fame
fate	feat	fume	fuse	game	gate	gems	gets	item
maes	mate	meat	mega	mesa	mets	mise	mite	muse
mute	safe	sage	same	sate	seam	seat	semi	seta
site	stem	suet	tame	team	teas	ties	time	

5 Letter Words

aegis	agues	amies	amuse	emits	fates	feast
feats	festa	fetus	fumes	games	gates	guest
guise	image	items	mates	meats	metus	mites
mutes	sitae	smite	stage	steam	suite	tames
teams	times	usage				

6 Letter Words

ageism, fiesta, images

7 Letter Words

fatigue, gamiest

8 Letter Words

fatigues, fumigate

9 Letter Words

fumigates

24

4 Letter Words — Words: 214

arts	bars	base	bass	bast	bats	bess	best	bets	boas	boss	bras	bros	burs	buss	bust
buts	ears	east	eats	eras	eros	esau	oars	oats	orbs	ores	ours	oust	outs	rase	rats
rest	reus	robs	roes	rose	rots	rubs	rues	ruse	rust	ruts	sale	sear	seas	seat	sera
serb	seta	sets	soar	sobs	sorb	sore	sort	sots	sour	sous	stab	star	stub	subs	sues
suet	sure	tabs	tars	teas	toes	toss	tubs	ures	user	uses	ussr				

5 Letter Words

abets	abuse	abuts	arose	asset	aster	autos	bares	baser	bases	baste	bates	bears
beast	beats	bests	betas	boars	boast	boats	boers	bores	bouts	braes	brass	brats
burst	buses	busts	oases	ousts	rases	rates	rebus	resat	rests	roast	robes	roses
rotas	rotes	rouse	roust	routs	rubes	ruses	rusts	saber	sabot	sates	sears	seato
seats	serbs	soars	sober	sorbs	sores	sorts	sours	souse	stabs	stare	stars	store
stubs	sutra	tares	taros	tears	tours	tress	trues	truss	tubas	tubes	users	

6 Letter Words

aborts	abuser	abuses	arouse	assert	assort	assure	asters	barest	basest	basset
bastes	beasts	boasts	bourse	breast	brutes	bursts	buster	obtuse	orates	ouster
rebuts	roasts	robust	roseau	rouses	rousts	routes	russet	sabers	sabots	sobers
sorbet	sorest	stares	stores	strobe	subset	surest	sutras	tabors	tarsus	tubers

7 Letter Words

abortus	abusers	arouses	boaster	boaters	bourses	breasts	busters	estrous
ousters	sorbets	sourest	strobes					

8 Letter Words

abstruse, boasters, saboteur

9 Letter Words

saboteurs

Solutions

25

4 Letter Words — **Words: 38**

alto, atop, clop, clot, coal, coat, coca, coil, cola, colt, copt, iota, loca, loci, opal, palo, plot, taco, toil

5 Letter Words

coati, colic, copal, octal, optic, patio, picot, pilot, plato, topic

6 Letter Words

calico, coital, coptic, pactio

7 Letter Words

capitol, optical, politic, topical

8 Letter Words

9 Letter Words

occipital

26

4 Letter Words — **Words: 16**

fill, fish, flow, foil, fowl, wolf

5 Letter Words

fills, filly, fishy, flows, foils, folly, fowls, wolfs

6 Letter Words

7 Letter Words

wolfish

8 Letter Words

9 Letter Words

wolfishly

27

4 Letter Words — **Words: 16**

newt, town, twin, view, went, wept, wine, wino, wipe, wont, wove

5 Letter Words

pewit, twine, woven

6 Letter Words

townie

7 Letter Words

8 Letter Words

9 Letter Words

viewpoint

28

4 Letter Words — **Words: 52**

eons, gens, gins, gnus, gone, guns, inns, ions, neon, nine, nisi, noes, none, nose, noun, nuns, ones, onus, sign, sine, sing, sinn, snug, song, sung

5 Letter Words

ennui, eosin, genii, genus, nines, nisei, noise, nouns, seign, singe, suing, sunni, union, using

6 Letter Words

ensign, geniis, genius, ginnie, nosing, unions, unison

7 Letter Words

ensuing, gunnies, igneous, noising, seining

8 Letter Words

9 Letter Words

ingenious

Solutions

29

4 Letter Words

deep	deft	dept	dies	diet	dieu	dues	duet
edit	efts	feed	fees	feet	fete	feud	fide
idee	ides	ipse	peed	pees	pest	pete	pets
pies	seed	seep	side	site	sped	step	sued
teed	tees	tide	tied	ties	used		

5 Letter Words

deeps	deist	diets	duets	dupes	edits	etude
feeds	feted	fetes	fetid	fetus	feuds	fides
fused	idees	pedis	piste	sited	speed	spied
spite	steed	steep	suede	suite	tepid	tides
upset						

6 Letter Words

defies	defuse	duties	espied	etudes	fisted
sifted	spited	suited	upside		

7 Letter Words

despite   dispute

8 Letter Words

deputies

9 Letter Words

stupefied

30

4 Letter Words

Words: 26

dupe	emus	gems	gums	mend	menu	mets	mugs	muse
fuse	must	mute	smug	smut	stem		
pied							
suet							

5 Letter Words

mends	menus	metus	mused	muted	mutes
sedum	unmet				

6 Letter Words

nutmeg   smudge

7 Letter Words

nutmegs

8 Letter Words

judgment

9 Letter Words

judgments

31

4 Letter Words

Words: 121

dels	dues	dust	eels	efts	else	fees	furs	fuse
lese	lest	lets	lust	reds	refs	rest	reus	rues
rust	ruts	seed	seer	self	sere	serf	sled	slue
slut	stud	sued	suet	surd	sure	surf	tees	ures
user								

5 Letter Words

duels	duets	durst	ester	feeds	feels	felts	fetes
fetus	feuds	flees	flues	frees	frets	fuels	furls
fused	fusel	fuser	leeds	leers	leets	lefts	lures
lutes	reeds	reefs	reels	reset	reuse	rules	seder
sleet	slued	steed	steel	steer	stele	suede	terse
trees	trues	turfs					

6 Letter Words

defers	defuse	desert	deters	duster	elders	eldest
eludes	elutes	etudes	fester	fleets	flutes	freest
lusted	luster	refuse	rested	result	reused	rudest
rusted	rustle	surfed	sutler	ulster		

7 Letter Words

duelers	ferules	fluster	refuels	refused	refutes
restful	rustled	strudel			

8 Letter Words

resulted

9 Letter Words

flustered

32

4 Letter Words

Words: 71

gate	gelt	halt	hart	hate	heat	late	lath	leet	lees
part	pate	path	peat	pelt	pert	pete	plat	leet	prat	ruse
rapt	rate	tale	tape	tare	tarp	teal	tear	trap	slur
tree									used

5 Letter Words

alert	alter	earth	eater	egret	elate	ethel
ether	garth	grate	great	greet	hater	heart
later	lathe	leapt	parte	pater	perth	petal
peter	plate	pleat	prate	taper	there	three

6 Letter Words

eaglet	gather	halter	heater	lather	legate
palter	petrel	reheat	relate	repeat	
freest					
rudest					

7 Letter Words

leather   preheat   prelate

9 Letter Words

telegraph

Solutions

33

4 Letter Words — Words: 37

aces, acne, cain, cane, cans, case, cues, cuss, ices, icus, inca, nice, nunc, sacs, scan

5 Letter Words

canes, cases, casus, cause, incas, sauce, scans, secus, since

6 Letter Words

canine, cannes, casein, causes, census, nuance, sauces, usance

7 Letter Words

canines, nuances

8 Letter Words

issuance, nuisance

9 Letter Words

nuisances

34

4 Letter Words — Words: 129

aced, aces, acne, acre, aden, area, cake, cane, care, case, cera, dace, dane, dare, dean, dear, deck, dens, desk, earn, ears, edna, ends, eras, near, neck, nerd, race, rake, rase, read, reck, reds, rend, sake, sane, sean, sear, send, sera

5 Letter Words

acres, andes, arced, arden, areas, arena, asked, cadre, caked, cakes, caned, canes, cared, cares, carne, cased, cedar, crake, crane, creak, daces, dance, danes, dares, deans, dears, decks, drake, earns, karen, knead, nacre, naked, nears, necks, nerds, raced, races, raked, rakes, rased, reads, recks, rends, saner, scare, sedan, snake, snare, sneak

6 Letter Words

andrea, arcade, arcane, arenas, ascend, cadres, caesar, canker, cedars, crakes, craned, cranes, creaks, dancer, dances, danker, darken, decana, drakes, kneads, nacres, racked, ranked, sacked, sacker, sacred, sander, scared, snaked, snared

7 Letter Words

arcades, askance, cankers, cranked, dancers, darkens, saracen, snacked

8 Letter Words

9 Letter Words

ransacked

35

4 Letter Words — Words: 131

akin, anew, ansi, gain, gens, gins, glen, gnaw, inks, kiln, king, klan, knew, lain, lane, lang, lank, lawn, lean, lens, lien, line, link, nags, nail, neil, news, nile, sane, sang, sank, sawn, sean, sewn, sign, sine, sing, sink, skin, snag, swan, wane, wang, wean, wens, wine, wing, wink, wins

5 Letter Words

agnes, alien, align, angel, angle, angli, anise, ankle, awing, eking, gains, glean, glens, gnaws, kilns, kings, lanes, lawns, leans, liens, liken, lines, links, nails, nigel, nikes, seign, signa, sinew, singe, skein, slain, slang, sling, slink, snail, snake, sneak, swain, swank, swine, swing, waken, wanes, weans, wines, wings, winks

6 Letter Words

aliens, aligns, angels, angles, ankles, asking, easing, genial, gleans, lesing, likens, saline, sawing, sewing, signal, silken, single, wakens, waking, wangle, winkle

7 Letter Words

leaking, leasing, linkage, sealing, skewing, slaking, walking, wangles, winkles

8 Letter Words

linkages, swanlike, weakling

9 Letter Words

weaklings

36

4 Letter Words — Words: 20

frog, giro, gong, grin, grog, ring

5 Letter Words

going, groin, vigor, virgo

6 Letter Words

firing, giving, goring, gringo, origin, riving, roving, virgin

7 Letter Words

forging

8 Letter Words

9 Letter Words

forgiving

Solutions

37

4 Letter Words — Words: 78

ahem, apes, apse, ease, east, eats, hate, heap, heat, hemp, hems, maes, mate, meat, meet, mesa, mese, mesh, mete, meth, mets, pate, peas, peat, pees, pest, pete, pets, same, sate, seam, seat, seem, seep, seta, seth, stem, step, tame, tape, team, teas, teem, tees, temp, them

5 Letter Words

haste, hates, heaps, heats, mates, meats, meets, metes, meths, paste, pates, phase, septa, setae, shame, shape, sheep, sheet, spate, steam, steep, tames, tapes, teams, tease, teems, temps, theme, these

6 Letter Words

peseta, themes

7 Letter Words

8 Letter Words

9 Letter Words

metaphase

38

4 Letter Words — Words: 84

ansi, anti, gain, gait, gins, gist, high, hint, hits, nigh, nits, shin, shit, sigh, sign, sine, sing, site, snit, thai, thin, this, ties, tina, tine, tins

5 Letter Words

aegis, agist, anise, antis, eight, entia, gains, gaits, giant, heist, highs, hinge, hints, inset, neigh, night, saint, satin, seign, shine, sight, signa, singe, singh, sitae, stain, stein, sting, thigh, thing, thins, tines, tinge

6 Letter Words

easing, eating, eighth, geisha, giants, hating, height, hinges, ingest, neighs, nights, sating, signet, thighs, things, tinges, tisane

7 Letter Words

eighths, hashing, heating, heights, highest, seating, teasing

8 Letter Words

9 Letter Words

sheathing

39

4 Letter Words — Words: 53

dent, done, eden, mend, morn, need, nemo, nerd, nero, node, nome, norm, note, omen, omne, rend, reno, rent, teen, tend, tent, tern, tone, torn

5 Letter Words

demon, dente, donee, drone, emend, enter, mente, monet, noted, onere, tenet, tenor, toned, toner, trend

6 Letter Words

dement, denote, mender, mentor, modern, netted, rented, rodent, rotten, tender, tented

7 Letter Words

mordent, torment

8 Letter Words

9 Letter Words

tormented

40

4 Letter Words — Words: 141

eire, erie, erin, fein, figs, fine, fins, fire, firs, fist, fits, gift, gins, girt, gist, grin, grit, nits, reif, rein, rien, rife, rift, rigs, ring, rise, rite, seri, sift, sign, sine, sing, sire, site, snit, stir, tier, ties, tine, tins, tire, trig

5 Letter Words

eigne, feign, feint, finer, fines, fires, first, fries, genie, gifts, grief, grins, grist, grits, inert, infer, inset, inter, irene, niger, refit, regis, regni, reign, reins, reits, resin, resit, retie, rifts, rings, rinse, risen, rites, seign, seine, serif, siege, singe, siren, stein, sting, tiers, tiger, tines, tinge, tires, tries, trigs, trine

6 Letter Words

engirt, entire, feigns, feints, feting, finest, finger, fregit, fringe, genies, infers, infest, ingest, insert, inters, refine, refits, reigns, resign, reties, rifest, seeing, sifter, signer, signet, singer, sinter, strife, string, teeing, teneri, tigers, tinges, trines

7 Letter Words

entries, fingers, freeing, fringes, generis, integer, reefing, refines, resting, snifter, stinger, treeing

8 Letter Words

integers, steering

9 Letter Words

festering

Solutions

41

Words: 198

4 Letter Words
dens, dies, dins, dips, dits, ends, ides, ipse, nest, nets, nips, nits, pees, pens, pest, pets, pies, pins, pits, pres, pris, reds, reps, rest, rids, rips, rise, seed, seen, seep, seer, send, sent, sere, seri, side, sine, sire, site, snip, snit, sped, spin, spit, step, stir, tees, tens, ties, tins, tips

5 Letter Words
deeps, deist, denis, dense, dents, diets, dines, dints, dries, drips, edits, ernst, ester, idees, inset, needs, nerds, pedis, peens, peers, pends, penis, perts, piers, pines, pints, piste, pries, reeds, reins, reits, rends, rents, reset, resin, resit, rides, rinds, rinse, risen, rites, seder, seine, sired, siren, sited, sneer, snide, snipe, speed, spend, spent, spied, spine, spire, spite, spree, sprit, steed, steep, steer, stein, stern, strip, teens, tends, tense, terns, terse, tides, tiers, tines, tires, trees, tries, trips

6 Letter Words
denies, denise, denser, desert, desire, deters, diners, direst, driest, eiders, enters, espied, esprit, insert, instep, inters, nested, nester, pester, peters, preens, prides, priest, prints, resent, reside, rested, reties, rinsed, ripens, ripest, seined, sender, sinter, snider, sniped, sniper, spider, spinet, spited, sprint, sprite, stride, stripe, tensed, tenser, trends, trines

7 Letter Words
deniers, despite, destine, dieters, entries, present, preside, reedits, repents, repines, respite, serpent, spender, stipend, striped, tenders

8 Letter Words
inserted, pretends, resident, sintered, sprinted, trendies

9 Letter Words
president

42

Words: 135

4 Letter Words
cent, coin, cone, cons, corn, eons, erin, icon, into, ions, iron, join, nero, nest, nets, nice, nits, noes, noir, nose, note, once, ones, rein, reno, rent, rien, sent, sine, snit, snot, tens, tern, tine, tins, tone, tons, torn

5 Letter Words
cents, coins, cones, corns, cosen, crone, eosin, ernst, icons, inert, inset, inter, intro, irons, joins, joint, jones, nicer, noire, noise, norse, notes, onset, reins, rents, resin, rinse, risen, rosin, scent, scion, scone, scorn, since, siren, snore, snort, sonic, stein, steno, stern, stone, tenor, terns, tines, toner, tones, tonic, trine

6 Letter Words
censor, citron, conies, cornet, cosine, cretin, crones, incest, inject, insect, insert, inters, intros, joiner, joints, nicest, nosier, notice, orient, oscine, rejoin, senior, sinter, tenors, tensor, tocsin, toners, tonics, trines

7 Letter Words
cistern, citroen, citrons, cornets, cretins, cronies, injects, joiners, jointer, notices, orients, rejoins, section, stonier

8 Letter Words
citroens, corniest, injector, jointers

9 Letter Words
injectors

43

Words: 55

4 Letter Words
emus, memo, menu, mets, moms, mono, moon, moos, moot, most, mote, mots, moue, mums, muse, must, mute, nemo, nome, noms, oems, omen, omne, smut, some, stem, sumo, tome, toms

5 Letter Words
memos, menus, meson, metus, monet, moons, moose, moots, motes, moues, mount, mouse, mutes, omens, omnes, smote, somme, tomes, unmet

6 Letter Words
moment, mounts, mouton, summon

7 Letter Words
moments, moutons

8 Letter Words

9 Letter Words
momentous

44

Words: 44

4 Letter Words
darn, ding, dung, gain, gang, grin, iran, pain, pang, ping, rain, rand, rang, rind, ring, ruin, rung

5 Letter Words
aging, aping, dinar, drain, grain, grand, grind, nadir, ruing

6 Letter Words
daring, duping, during, gaping, paging, paring, purina, raging, raping, unpaid, urging

7 Letter Words
arguing, draping, grading, niggard, purging

8 Letter Words
guarding

9 Letter Words
upgrading

Solutions

45

Words: 84

4 Letter Words

gels, gelt, gens, gent, gets, glen, isle, legs, leis, lens, lent, lest, lets, lien, lies, line, lite, neil, nest, nets, nile, nine, sent, sine, site, tens, ties, tile, tine

5 Letter Words

genii, gents, glenn, glens, inlet, inset, intel, islet, legit, lenin, liens, linen, lines, nigel, nines, nisei, seign, singe, stein, stile, tiles, tines, tinge

6 Letter Words

enlist, ensign, geniis, ginnie, ignite, ingest, inlets, lesing, linens, linnet, listen, signet, silent, single, tennis, tinges, tingle, tinsel

7 Letter Words

glisten, ignites, lignite, linnets, nesting, seining, tensing, tingles

8 Letter Words

ensiling, leninist, nestling

9 Letter Words

enlisting, listening, tinseling

46

Words: 144

4 Letter Words

acte, acts, arts, cart, cast, cats, cite, coat, cost, cots, crts, east, eats, iota, oats, rate, rats, rest, riot, rite, ritz, rota, rote, rots, sate, scat, scot, seat, sect, seta, site, soit, sort, star, stir, taco, tare, taro, tars, tear, teas, tics, tier, ties, tire, toes, tore, trio, tzar, zest, zits

5 Letter Words

actes, actor, artis, ascot, aster, astir, aztec, caret, carte, carts, caste, cater, certi, cista, cites, coast, coati, coats, costa, crate, crest, croat, irate, orate, rates, ratio, react, recta, recti, recto, reits, resat, resit, riots, rites, roast, rotas, rotes, scite, seato, sitae, sitar, stair, stare, stoic, store, tacos, tares, taros, tarsi, tears, tiers, tires, trace, trice, tries, trios, tzars

6 Letter Words

actors, aortic, carets, caster, castor, castro, caters, coatis, corset, cortis, crates, croats, erotic, ersatz, escort, orates, racist, ratios, reacts, recast, rectos, satire, scoter, scotia, scrota, sector, sortie, stacie, tories, traces

7 Letter Words

coaster, erotica, raciest

8 Letter Words

craziest

9 Letter Words

ostracize

47

Words: 125

4 Letter Words

aced, acid, adds, aden, adit, aide, aids, ands, cads, dace, dads, dais, dane, date, dead, dean, dedi, dens, dent, dica, dice, died, dies, diet, dine, dins, dint, disc, dits, edit, edna, ends, enid, iced, idea, ides, inde, said, sand, send, side, tads, tend, tide, tied

5 Letter Words

acids, acted, addis, adits, aided, aides, andes, anted, aside, cadet, caned, cased, cedit, cited, daces, dance, danes, dante, dated, dates, deans, deist, dends, denis, dents, diane, diced, dices, dicta, diets, dined, dines, dints, edict, edits, ideas, sated, sedan, sided, sited, snide, staid, stand, stead, tends, tided, tides, tined

6 Letter Words

addict, ascend, caddie, caddis, cadets, candid, canted, danced, dances, decani, decant, detain, edicts, sadden, sanded, standi

7 Letter Words

addicts, caddies, candied, candies, dandies, decants, descant, detains, distend, instead, sainted, scanted, stained

8 Letter Words

dandiest, distance

9 Letter Words

distanced

48

Words: 25

4 Letter Words

chug, gaul, haul, hula, hung, lung, nunc, ulan, ulna

5 Letter Words

annul, clung, gulch, laugh, lucia, lunch

6 Letter Words

annuli, launch, lingua, lucian, uncial

7 Letter Words

hauling, unchain

8 Letter Words

lunching, unlacing

9 Letter Words

launching

Solutions

49

4 Letter Words

eros	hero	hoes	home	hors	hose	host	hots	hour	hove	
mhos	more	mors	mort	most	mote	moth	mots	moue	move	
oems	ohms	ores	ours	oust	outs	over	ovum	roes	rome	
rose	rosh	rote	rots	rout	rove	shoe	shot	some	sore	
sort	sour	sumo	toes	tome	toms	tore	tour	veto	vote	

5 Letter Words

ethos	homer	homes	horse	hours	house	hover	humor
metro	mores	morse	motes	moths	moues	mouse	mouth
mover	moves	other	outer	overs	overt	rotes	rouse
roust	route	routs	roves	servo	shore	short	shout
shove	smote	south	store	storm	stove	those	throe
tomes	tours	trove	tumor	verso	voter	votes	

6 Letter Words

homers	hovers	humors	metros	mother	mouser	mouths
movers	others	ouster	routes	shrove	strove	throes
throve	troves	tumors	voters			

7 Letter Words

mothers   shouter   smother   thermos

8 Letter Words

vermouth

9 Letter Words

vermouths

50

Words: 121

4 Letter Words

ails	alit	iota	iowa	ital	kilo	kilt	kist	
kits	lisa	list	oils	sail	silk	silo	silt	
skit	slit	soil	soit	soli	tail	tilt	tits	
toil	twit	wail	wait	wilt	wits			

5 Letter Words

kilos	kilts	kitts	stilt	tails	tilts
toils	twist	twits	wails	waist	waits
wilts					

6 Letter Words

taoist

7 Letter Words

8 Letter Words

kilowatt

9 Letter Words

kilowatts

Words: 46

51

52

Solutions

53

4 Letter Words
mice   mien   mime   mine   nice   nine

Words: 11

5 Letter Words
mince   niece

6 Letter Words
icemen   nicene

7 Letter Words

8 Letter Words

9 Letter Words
imminence

54

4 Letter Words

Words: 105

eire	erie	erin	gins	girt	gist	grin	grit	nits
rein	rien	rigs	ring	rise	rite	seri	sign	sine
sing	sire	site	snit	stir	tier	ties	tine	tins
tint	tire	tits	trig					

5 Letter Words

eigne	genie	grins	grist	grits	inert	inset
inter	irene	niger	regis	regni	reign	reins
reits	resin	resit	retie	rings	rinse	risen
rites	seign	seine	siege	singe	siren	stein
sting	stint	tiers	tiger	tines	tinge	tints
tires	tries	trigs	trine	trite		

6 Letter Words

engirt	entire	genies	ingest	insert	inters
reigns	resign	reties	seeing	signer	signet
singer	sinter	sitter	string	teeing	teneri
tigers	tinges	trines			

7 Letter Words
entries   generis   integer   resting   setting
stinger   testier   testing   treeing

8 Letter Words
integers   interest   steering

9 Letter Words
resetting

55

4 Letter Words

Words: 156

alps aped apes aprs apse daps dope drop epos lapp laps leap lope lops opal pads
pale palo pals pard pare paso peal pear peas peps peso plea pled plod plop pods
pole pope pops pore pose ppos prep pres prod prop pros rape raps rasp reap repo
reps rope slap slop soap spar sped

5 Letter Words

aesop apple doper dopes drape drops lapse leaps loped lopes opals opera padre
paled paler pales paper pared pares parol parse peals pearl pears pedal plead
pleas plods plops polar poled poles popes pored pores posed poser preps prods
prole props prose raped rapes reaps repos roped ropes sepal slope spade spare
spear spore

6 Letter Words

aleppo apples dapper dapple dopers drapes lapped lapsed lopped operas padres
papers parole parsed pearls pedals peplos pleads polder poplar proles propel
rapped rappel rasped sapped sapper sloped soaped sopped spared spread

7 Letter Words
apposer   dapples   doppler   leopard   paroled   paroles   polders   poplars   presold
propels   rappels   slapped   slopped

8 Letter Words
leopards

9 Letter Words
prolapsed

56

4 Letter Words

Words: 160

aden ante dale dane dare date deal dean dear deer dent duel duet dune dure earl
earn eden edna etna lade lane late lead lean leer leet lend lent lure lute near
neat need nerd nude rate read reae real reed reel rend rent rude rued rule rune
tale tare teal tear teed teen tend tern tree tune unde urea

5 Letter Words

adler alder alert alter anted arden autre dante dealt delta dente deter eared
eaten eater eland elate elder elude elute endue enter enure etude laden later
laude leant learn lured rated renal ruled trade tread treed trend trued tuned
tuner ulnae under

6 Letter Words

antler ardent darnel dealer dental dueler earned elated eluted endear endure
enured lateen lauren leaden leader leaned leaner learnt lender nature neared
neater neural neuter ranted relate relent rental rented runlet tender tenure
propel tureen turned unread unreal unreel

7 Letter Words
alerted   altered   denture   durante   eternal   launder   learned   natured   naturel
neutral   related   renault   tenured   treadle   trundle

8 Letter Words
antlered   denature   underlet

9 Letter Words
unaltered   unrelated

Solutions

57

4 Letter Words
berg bern bier brie brig ergs erin fern fire
firs grin iris refs reif rein ribs rien rife
rigs ring rise serb serf seri sire

5 Letter Words
bergs biers brief brigs brine bring ferns
fiber fieri finer fires fries grief grins
infer niger regii regis regni reign reins
resin rings rinse risen serif siren

6 Letter Words
bering briefs brines brings fibers fibrin
finger firing fringe infers reigns resign
rising signer singer siring

7 Letter Words
fingers firings fringes

8 Letter Words
briefing

9 Letter Words
briefings

58

Words: 73

4 Letter Words
aver over rave revs rove save vase vast
vats vest veto vets vote

5 Letter Words
avers avert favor fovea ovate overs
overt raves roves saver savor servo
soave stave stove trove versa verso
voter votes

6 Letter Words
averts favors starve strove troves
vaster voters

7 Letter Words

8 Letter Words

9 Letter Words
overstaff

59

4 Letter Words
ergo erin girl giro gore greg grin grog
lire lore lori nero noir ogre over rein
rien rile ring rive roil role rove voir

5 Letter Words
giver goner gorge grieg groin grove liner
liver loire loner lover negro niger noire
oiler regni reign riven vigor viler vireo
virge virgo

6 Letter Words
ginger glover goring govern gringo grovel
ignore lienor linger logger longer nigger
region renvoi roving

7 Letter Words
verging

8 Letter Words

9 Letter Words
groveling

60

Words: 77

4 Letter Words
aden aide akin aped arid dane dank dare dark
darn dean dear earn edna idea iran nape nark
iron neap near paid pain pair pane pard pare park
reno peak pear raid rain rake rand rank rape read
reap ripa

5 Letter Words
aider aired arden diane dinar drain drake
drank drape karen knead nadir naked padre
paned paper pared prank raked raped rapid

6 Letter Words
append danker dapper darken diaper kidnap
napped pained paired pander parked rained
ranked rapine rapped repaid

7 Letter Words
prepaid

8 Letter Words

9 Letter Words
kidnapper

Solutions

61

4 Letter Words

adit, arts, dart, date, diet, dirt, dits, drat, east, eats, edit, rate, rats, rest, rite, sate, seat, seta, site, star, stew, stir, swat, tads, tare, tars, taws, tear, teas, teed, tees, tide, tied, tier, ties, tire, tree, wait, wart, west, wets, wits, writ

5 Letter Words

adits, artis, aster, astir, darts, dates, deist, deter, diets, eater, edits, ester, irate, rated, rates, reits, resat, reset, resit, retie, rites, sated, setae, sitae, sitar, sited, staid, stair, stare, stead, steed, steer, straw, strew, sweat, sweet, tares, tarsi, tears, tease, terse, tides, tiers, tired, tires, trade, tread, treed, trees, triad, tried, tries, tweed, waist, waits, warts, waste, water, wrest, wrist, write, writs

6 Letter Words

desert, deters, dieter, direst, driest, easter, eaters, ideate, rawest, reedit, rested, retied, reties, satire, seated, sedate, stared, stewed, stride, teased, teaser, tiered, tirade, trades, treads, triads, tweeds, wadset, waited, waiter, wasted, waster, waters, widest, wriest, writes

7 Letter Words

astride, dearest, dewiest, dieters, disrate, ideates, reedits, steward, strewed, sweater, tirades, waiters, wariest, watered, wrested

8 Letter Words

readiest, steadier, sweatier, weariest, weirdest

9 Letter Words

waterside

62

Words: 162

4 Letter Words

hems, home, homo, mesh, mess, meth, mets, mhos, moos, moot, moss, most, mote, moth, mots, oems, ohms, some, stem, them, tome, toms

5 Letter Words

homes, meths, moose, moots, moses, motes, motet, moths, motto, smote, stems, tomes, totem

6 Letter Words

motets, mottos, smooth, totems

7 Letter Words

mottoes

8 Letter Words

smoothes

9 Letter Words

smoothest

63

4 Letter Words

Words: 13

fogy, font, info, into, tong, tony, yogi

5 Letter Words

ingot

6 Letter Words

notify, noting, toning, toying

7 Letter Words

8 Letter Words

9 Letter Words

notifying

64

4 Letter Words

Words: 34

beck, chew, chow, coke, cone, conk, core, cork, corn, crew, crow, echo, heck, hock, neck, once, reck, rock

5 Letter Words

bench, choke, chore, cohen, cower, crone, crown, enoch, ochre, wench, wreck

6 Letter Words

beckon, choker, reckon, wrench

7 Letter Words

8 Letter Words

9 Letter Words

workbench

Solutions

65

Words: 60

4 Letter Words
emus, eons, mets, moms, most, mots, mums, muse, must, nest, nets, noes, noms, nose, nuns, nuts, oems, ones, onus, oust, outs, sent, smut, snot, some, stem, stun, suet, sumo, tens, toes, toms, tons, tuns

5 Letter Words
memos, menus, meson, metus, motes, moues, mouse, mutes, notes, nouns, omens, omnes, onset, smote, snout, somme, steno, stone, tomes, tones, tunes

6 Letter Words
mounts, sonnet, summon

7 Letter Words
moments

8 Letter Words

9 Letter Words
monuments

66

Words: 84

4 Letter Words
eons, eros, leon, lone, lore, lose, love, lyon, nero, noel, noes, nose, nosy, ones, only, onus, ores, ours, oven, over, oyer, reno, roes, role, rose, rosy, rove, sloe, sole, sony, sore, soul, sour, vole, yore, your

5 Letter Words
envoy, loner, loser, louse, lousy, lover, loves, lyons, noels, norse, nosey, novel, novus, ovens, overs, ovule, oyers, roles, rouen, rouse, roves, seoul, servo, snore, solve, verso, voles, yours

6 Letter Words
envoys, loners, louver, louvre, lovers, novels, overly, ovules, solver, sorely, sourly, velour, venous, volens, voyeur

7 Letter Words
louvers, louvres, nervous, voyeurs

8 Letter Words

9 Letter Words
nervously

67

Words: 52

4 Letter Words
dent, dine, dint, eden, enid, erin, hind, hint, inde, need, nerd, rein, rend, rent, rien, rind, teen, tend, tern, then, thin, tine

5 Letter Words
dente, diner, enter, hindi, inert, inter, irene, rhine, tined, trend, trine

6 Letter Words
denier, entire, herein, hinder, hinted, inhere, nether, reined, rented, tender, teneri, tinder, tinier

7 Letter Words
inhered, inherit, neither, nitride, therein

8 Letter Words

9 Letter Words
inherited

68

Words: 191

4 Letter Words
ante, earn, ears, east, eats, eons, eras, eros, etna, hare, hate, hear, heat, hens, hero, hers, hoes, hone, hose, near, neat, nero, nest, nets, noes, nose, note, ones, ores, rase, rate, reno, rent, rest, rhea, roes, rose, rote, sane, sate, sean, sear, seat, sent, sera, seta, seth, shoe, sore, stet, tare, tear, teas, teat, tens, tent, tern, test, then, toes, tone, tore, tote

5 Letter Words
antes, arose, ashen, aster, atone, earns, earth, eaton, ernst, ethos, hanse, hares, haste, hater, hates, hears, heart, heats, heron, hones, horae, horse, hosea, nears, norse, notae, notes, oaten, onset, orate, other, otter, rates, rents, resat, rheas, rhone, rotes, saner, seato, shane, share, shear, shone, shore, snare, snore, stare, state, steno, stern, stone, store, tares, taste, tears, teats, tenor, tenth, tents, terns, tetra, thane, theta, those, throe, toner, tones, torte, totes, treat

6 Letter Words
anther, ashore, astern, athens, atones, earths, hasten, haters, hatter, hearts, herons, hoarse, honest, hornet, hotter, natter, orates, ornate, others, otters, reason, rotate, rotten, stante, staten, sterna, taster, tehran, tenors, tensor, tenths, tetras, thanes, thetas, threat, throes, throne, toners, tortes, treats

7 Letter Words
another, anthers, earshot, hatters, hornets, natters, rotates, senator, shatter, shorten, threats, thrones, toaster, treason

8 Letter Words
rheostat, sheraton

9 Letter Words
northeast

Solutions

69

4 Letter Words

aden, ands, ante, ants, arts, dane, dare, darn, dart, dash, date, dean, dear, drat, earn, ears, ease, east, eats, edna, eras, etna, hand, hard, hare, hart, hate, hats, head, hear, heat, near, neat, rand, rant, rase, rash, rate, rats, read, reae, rhea, sand, sane, sate, sean, sear, seat, sera, seta, shad, shat, stan, star, tads, tans, tare, tars, tear, teas, than

5 Letter Words

andes, anted, antes, arden, ashen, aster, danes, dante, dares, darns, darts, dates, deans, dears, death, eared, earns, earth, eased, eaten, eater, erase, hades, hands, hanse, hared, hares, harts, haste, hated, hater, hates, heads, heard, hears, heart, heats, nears, rands, rants, rased, rated, rates, reads, resat, rheas, saner, sated, sedan, setae, shade, shane, shard, share, shear, snare, stand, stare, stead, tares, tears, tease, thane, trade, trash, tread

6 Letter Words

adhere, anther, ardent, astern, athens, dasher, dearth, deaths, earned, earths, easter, eaters, endear, erased, ethane, hander, harden, hasten, haters, hatred, header, hearse, hearts, heated, heater, neared, neater, ranted, reheat, sander, sateen, seared, seated, sedate, senate, shared, snared, stared, sterna, strand, teased, teaser, tehran, thanes, thread, trades, treads

7 Letter Words

adheres, anthers, dearest, earnest, earthed, earthen, eastern, endears, handers, handset, hardens, hardest, hatreds, headers, headset, hearted, hearten, heaters, nearest, reheats, sheared, standee, teheran, theresa, threads, trashed

8 Letter Words

adherent, hastened, headrest, heartens

9 Letter Words

adherents

70

Words: 205

4 Letter Words

eels, ells, else, ills, isle, lees, leet, leis, lens, lent, leon, lese, lest, lets, lien, lies, lilt, line, lint, lion, list, lite, loin, lone, lose, lost, lots, neil, nile, noel, oils, olin, sell, sill, silo, silt, slit, sloe, slot, soil, sole, soli, tell, tile, till, toil, toll

5 Letter Words

elise, elite, ellen, elsie, inlet, intel, intol, islet, leets, lento, liens, lilts, lines, lions, lisle, loins, noels, nolle, sleet, solet, steel, stele, stile, still, stole, tells, tiles, tills, toile, toils, tolls

6 Letter Words

enlist, ensile, inlets, insole, lentil, lentos, lesion, leslie, lintel, listen, nestle, senile, silent, stolen, tinsel, tonsil

7 Letter Words

lentils, lintels, tensile

8 Letter Words

9 Letter Words

loneliest

71

Words: 133

4 Letter Words

ager, ages, ails, airs, ales, aril, aver, earl, ears, ella, eras, gael, gail, gale, gall, gals, gars, gave, gear, ilea, iras, lags, lair, lave, leal, leas, liar, lira, lisa, rage, rags, rail, rase, rave, real, rial, riga, sage, sail, sale, sari, save, seal, sear, sera, slag, slav, vale, vase, veal, vela, vial, visa

5 Letter Words

aegis, agers, agile, aires, aisle, alive, argil, aries, arils, arise, arles, avers, earls, elias, gaels, gales, galls, gavel, gears, glare, grail, grave, lager, lairs, large, laser, laves, legal, liars, liras, rages, rails, raise, ravel, raves, regal, rials, rival, sager, salve, saver, slave, vegas, velar, versa, vials, villa, viral

6 Letter Words

allies, argils, gavels, glares, grails, graves, gravis, israel, lagers, ligare, ravels, rivals, sallie, salver, serial, silage, slaver, valise, varies, velars, villas, visage

7 Letter Words

algiers, gravies, legalis, rallies, regalis, revisal, village

8 Letter Words

villager, villages

9 Letter Words

villagers

72

Words: 48

4 Letter Words

aims, alma, alms, gams, lama, lams, lima, limn, magi, mail, main, mala, mali, mans, mils, nama, siam, slam, slim, viam

5 Letter Words

anima, gamin, islam, lamas, limas, limns, magna, mails, mains, mania, milan, salmi, sigma

6 Letter Words

animal, animas, gamins, lamina, laming, malian, malign, manias, manila, salami

7 Letter Words

animals, laminas, maligns, manilas

8 Letter Words

9 Letter Words

galvanism

Solutions

73

Words: 137

4 Letter Words
acre aprs arch arcs care carp cars cera char crap cure curs ears ecru
eras errs hare harp hear hers pare pear peru pres pure purr race rape
raps rare rase rash rasp reap rear reps reus rhea rues ruse rush scar
sear sera spar spur sure urea ures user

5 Letter Words
acres caper cares carpe carps chars crape craps crash cruse crush
curae cures curse hares harps hears pacer parch pares parse pears
perch purer purrs purse racer races rapes reach reaps rears recap
recur rheas ruche scare scarp scrap share sharp shear spare spear
super supra surer usher

6 Letter Words
archer arches capers carper chaser crapes curare pacers parsec
parser phrase preach purser pusher racers rasher rasure recaps
recurs ruches rusher saucer scrape search seraph shaper sharer
spacer sparer spruce

7 Letter Words
archers crasher crusher parches scarper scraper sharper

8 Letter Words
purchase

9 Letter Words
purchaser

74

Words: 254

4 Letter Words
ales aver earl ears ease east eats eels eire else eras erie ever eves evil ilea
isle late lave leas leer lees leet leis lese lest lets levi lies lire lite live
rase rate rave reae real reel rest revs rile rise rite rive sale sate save seal
sear seat seer sera sere seri seta sire site sive tale tare teal tear teas tees
tier ties tile tire tree vale vase veal veer veil vela vest vets vies vile

5 Letter Words
aires aisle alert alive alter aries arise arles aster avers avert earls easel
eater eaves elate elias elise elite elsie elves elvis erase ester evils irate
islet laser later laves lease least leave leers leets lever liter liver lives
raise rates ravel raves reels reits resat reset resit retie revel riles rites
rives rivet salve saver serve setae sever sieve sitae slate slave sleet slier
stale stare stave steal steel steer stele steve stile tales tares teals tears
tease terse tiers tiler tiles tires trees tries valet veers veies veils velar
versa verse viler vires vitae

6 Letter Words
alerts aliter alters averse averts easier easter eaters elates israel leaves
levers levies lister litera liters livers ravels relate relies relive resale
reseal retail reties reveal reveils revest revile revise rivets salver satire
sealer serial silver slaver sliver staler starve strive svelte teasel teaser
tilers travel valets valise varies vaster velars verist vestal vilest

7 Letter Words
atelier literae realest realist relates relives restive retails reveals
reviles revisal saltier servile several stealer sterile travels valerie
veritas

8 Letter Words
ateliers earliest realties relative

9 Letter Words
relatives versatile

75

Words: 44

4 Letter Words
adds ands dads darn doll dons dora lads
land lard load lord nods odds olds rand
road rods sand soda sold

5 Letter Words
adorn darns dolls dorsa droll lands
lards loads lords nodal radon rands
roads

6 Letter Words
adorns arnold dollar donald dorsal
roland ronald

7 Letter Words
dollars

8 Letter Words
landlord

9 Letter Words
landlords

76

Words: 60

4 Letter Words
deer doer dred herd here hero horn nerd nero
redo reed rend reno rent rode rote tern tore
torn tree trod

5 Letter Words
deter drone enter erode ether heron horde
north odder onere other rhode rhone tenor
there thorn three throe toner treed trend

6 Letter Words
droned eroded herded hereon hereto horned
hornet nether redden rented rodent tender
throne

7 Letter Words
thereon trended trodden

8 Letter Words
dethrone

9 Letter Words
dethroned

Solutions

77

4 Letter Words

deem drum emus mere mers mese mess muse
rums seem sums

5 Letter Words

deems demur drums mused muses rerum
sedum seems serum

6 Letter Words

demure demurs messed murder mussed
resume serums

7 Letter Words

demurer murders resumed resumes

8 Letter Words

9 Letter Words

murderess

78

Words: 32

4 Letter Words

emir	erin	ions	ious	iron	mien	mine	mire	mise
nevi	noir	rein	rien	rime	rims	rise	rive	ruin
semi	seri	sine	sire	sive	vein	vies	vine	voir

5 Letter Words

emirs	envoi	eosin	inure	irons	miens	miner
mines	minor	minus	mires	miser	movie	nevis
noire	noise	omnis	osier	ovine	reims	reins
resin	rimes	rinse	risen	riven	rives	rosin
ruins	simon	siren	urine	veins	vines	vireo
vires	virus	visne	visor			

6 Letter Words

envois	insure	inures	isomer	merino	miners
minors	moines	movies	nosier	renvoi	senior
ursine	verism	vermin	vinous	vireos	

7 Letter Words

envious merinos mousier renvois version

8 Letter Words

monsieur souvenir

9 Letter Words

verminous

79

Words: 4

4 Letter Words

rind whir

5 Letter Words

whirl

6 Letter Words

7 Letter Words

8 Letter Words

9 Letter Words

whirlwind

80

Words: 119

4 Letter Words

acts	anti	ants	arts	cant	cart	cast	cats	coat	cost
cots	crts	into	iota	nato	nits	nota	oats	rant	rats
riot	rota	rots	scat	scot	snit	snot	soit	sort	stan
star	stir	taco	tans	taro	tars	tics	tina	tins	tons
torn	trio								

5 Letter Words

actin	actor	antic	antis	artis	ascot	astir	aston
cacti	canto	cants	carts	cista	coast	coati	coats
costa	croat	intra	intro	rants	ratio	riots	roast
rotas	saint	santo	satin	scant	sitar	snort	stain
stair	stoic	tacos	taros	tarsi	tonic	train	trios

6 Letter Words

accost	action	actors	antics	aortic	arctic	cantor
cantos	carton	castor	castro	citron	coatis	contra
cortis	croats	instar	intros	racist	ration	ratios
scotia	scrota	strain	tocsin	tonics	trains	

7 Letter Words

actions cantors cartons citrons contras rations

8 Letter Words

acrostic narcotic socratic

9 Letter Words

narcotics

Solutions

81

4 Letter Words — Words: 8
whys   will   wily   wish

5 Letter Words
swill   wills

6 Letter Words

7 Letter Words
wishful

8 Letter Words

9 Letter Words
wishfully

82

4 Letter Words — Words: 39
aide   arid   dedi   died   dire   hair   heir   hide
hire   idea   raid   ride   weir   whir   wide   wire

5 Letter Words
aided   aider   aired   direr   dried   drier
hired   hirer   redid   rider   weird   wider
wired   wrier

6 Letter Words
haired   raided   raider   warier

7 Letter Words
hardier   harried   rawhide   whirred

8 Letter Words

9 Letter Words
hardwired

83

4 Letter Words — Words: 100
also   alto   blot   boar   boas   boat   bola   bolo   bolt
boor   boos   boot   boss   bros   laos   lobo   lobs   loot
loss   lost   lots   oars   oats   oral   orbs   oslo   robs
root   rota   rots   slob   slot   soar   sobs   sola   solo
soot   sorb   sort   sots   taro   tool   toss

5 Letter Words
abort   altos   bator   bloat   blots   boars   boast
boats   bolas   bolos   bolts   boors   boost   boots
labor   lasso   lobar   lobos   loots   orals   roast
robot   roost   roots   rotas   sabot   slobs   slots
soars   solar   solos   sorbs   sorts   stool   taboo
tabor   taros   tools   torso

6 Letter Words
aborts   assort   bloats   boasts   boosts   labors
roasts   robots   roosts   sabots   stools   taboos
tabors   torsos

7 Letter Words
toolbar

8 Letter Words
barstool   toolbars

9 Letter Words
barstools

84

4 Letter Words — Words: 35
gene   gens   gent   glen   hens   lens   lent   nest
nets   seen   sent   teen   tens   then
loot   robs
solo

5 Letter Words
genes   genet   gents   ghent   glenn   glens
helen   sheen   teens   tense

6 Letter Words
genets   gentes   gentle   length   lenten
nestle   tenens

7 Letter Words
gentles   lengths

8 Letter Words
lengthen

9 Letter Words
lengthens

Solutions

85

Words: 85

4 Letter Words

ears, eras, eros, ewer, hare, hear, here, hero, hora, hors, hour, oars, ores, ours, rase, rash, reus, rhea, roes, rose, rosh, rows, rues, ruse, sear, seer, sera, sere, soar, sore, sour, sure, ures, user, ware, wars, wear, were, wore

5 Letter Words

arose, erase, ewers, hares, hears, heres, hewer, horae, horse, hours, reuse, rheas, rouse, sewer, share, shear, sheer, shore, shrew, sower, swear, swore, usher, wares, wears, where, whore, worse

6 Letter Words

arouse, ashore, hawser, hearse, heroes, hewers, hoarse, roseau, shower, washer, whores

7 Letter Words

rehouse, whereas

8 Letter Words

9 Letter Words

warehouse

86

Words: 57

4 Letter Words

cite, coil, eric, lice, lieu, lire, lite, loci, lori, hers, rice, rico, rile, riot, rite, roil, tier, tile, tire, reae, rush, toil, trio, uric, urea

5 Letter Words

certi, crier, curie, curio, licet, liter, loire, louie, oiler, oleic, recti, relic, ricer, tiler, tirol, toile, trice, trier, trior, ureic, uteri, utile

6 Letter Words

currit, erotic, loiter, lucite, recoil, relict, rioter, toiler

7 Letter Words

courier, curlier, recruit

8 Letter Words

courtier, ulterior

9 Letter Words

courtlier

87

Words: 55

4 Letter Words

bend, bled, bred, deed, deer, dred, drub, dude, duel, dune, dure, eden, lend, need, nerd, nude, reed, rend, rude, rued, unde

5 Letter Words

bedel, bleed, blend, breed, elder, elude, ended, endue, lured, ruled, udder, under

6 Letter Words

bender, bundle, burden, burned, delude, denude, dueled, dueler, dundee, eluded, endued, endure, enured, lender, redden

7 Letter Words

blended, blender, blunder, bundled, endured

8 Letter Words

burdened

9 Letter Words

blundered

88

Words: 138

4 Letter Words

ales, aloe, alps, also, aryl, earl, laos, laps, lave, laye, lays, leap, leas, levy, lope, lops, lore, lose, love, lyre, opal, oral, oval, pale, palo, pals, peal, play, plea, ploy, pole, poly, real, rely, role, sale, seal, slap, slav, slay, sloe, slop, sola, sole, vale, veal, vela, vole, yale, yelp

5 Letter Words

aloes, arles, aryls, earls, early, lapse, laser, laves, layer, leaps, lopes, loser, lover, loves, lyres, opals, orals, ovals, paler, pales, palsy, parol, peals, pearl, plays, pleas, ploys, polar, poles, prole, ravel, relay, reply, roles, royal, salve, salvo, sepal, slave, slope, slyer, solar, solve, splay, valor, velar, voles, yelps

6 Letter Words

layers, loaves, lovers, overly, parley, parole, pearls, pearly, player, plover, proles, ravels, relays, replay, salver, salvor, slaver, slayer, solver, sorely, valero, velars

7 Letter Words

layover, leprosy, overlap, overlay, parleys, paroles, parsley, players, plovers, replays, saveloy, slavery, sparely

8 Letter Words

layovers, overlaps, overlays, overplay

9 Letter Words

overplays

Solutions

89

4 Letter Words

ante	ants	east	eats	etna	mast	mate	mats	meat
meet	mete	mets	neat	nest	nets	sate	seat	sent
seta	sets	stan	stem	stet	tame	tams	tans	tats
team	teas	teat	teem	teen	tees	tens	tent	test

5 Letter Words

antes	asset	eaten	masts	mates	matte	meant
meats	meets	mente	metes	nests	sates	seats
setae	state	steam	stems	stets	tames	taste
teams	tease	teats	teems	teens	tenet	tense
tents	teste	tests				

6 Letter Words

assent	estate	mattes	sanest	sateen	senate
sestet	stamen	stante	staten	states	steams
tamest	tastes	teases	tenets	tenses	testes
tsetse					

7 Letter Words

estates	meanest	neatest	senates	sensate
stamens	tensest			

8 Letter Words

tameness

9 Letter Words

statesmen

90

Words: 48

4 Letter Words

come	corm	meow	mere	mers	mese	mews	more
morn	mors	mown	mows	nemo	nome	noms	norm
oems	omen	omne	rome	seem	some	worm	

5 Letter Words

comer	comes	corms	creme	meows	mesne
meson	mores	morns	morse	mower	norms
omens	omnes	semen	women	worms	

6 Letter Words

comers	cowmen	mowers	sermon

7 Letter Words

crewmen   emerson

8 Letter Words

newcomer

9 Letter Words

newcomers

91

Words: 95 (for 89)

4 Letter Words

anti	ants	gait	gast	gatt	gist	gnat	nits	snit
stag	stan	tags	tang	tans	tats	tina	tins	tint
tits								

5 Letter Words

agist	angst	antis	gaits	giant	gnats	saint
satin	stain	sting	stint	taint	tangs	tints
titan						

6 Letter Words

giants	sating	siting	taints	titans	titian

7 Letter Words

instant	signati	sitting	stating	tasting
tinting			

8 Letter Words

staining	stinting	tainting

9 Letter Words

instating

92

Words: 59

4 Letter Words

alit	anti	aunt	gait	gilt	glut	gnat	halt	haut
hilt	hint	hunt	ital	lath	lint	tail	tang	thai
than	thin	thug	tina	tiny	tuna	unit	utah	

5 Letter Words

aught	aunty	gault	gaunt	giant	glint	guilt
haunt	italy	laity	latin	light	night	tangy
thing	tying	uniat	unity	unlit	until	

6 Letter Words

alight	guilty	hating	litany	naught	nighty
thinly	tingly			

7 Letter Words

gauntly	halting	naughty	nightly

8 Letter Words

9 Letter Words

naughtily

Solutions

93

4 Letter Words

ally, ella, fall, feal, fell, flak, flaw, flay, flea, flew, flue, fuel, full, kale, kyle, lake, laye, leaf, leak, leal, luke, wale, walk, wall, weal, well, yale, yawl, yell, yule

5 Letter Words

alkyl, alley, awful, flake, flaky, fluke, fluky, fully, kelly, leafy, leaky, wally

6 Letter Words

lawful, weakly

7 Letter Words

awfully, wakeful

8 Letter Words

9 Letter Words

wakefully

94

Words: 47

4 Letter Words

airy, aril, gail, gain, girl, grin, iran, jail, lain, lair, liar, lira, nail, rail, rain, rial, riga, ring

5 Letter Words

align, angli, argil, gaily, grail, grain, inlay, lying, rainy, riyal

6 Letter Words

grainy, laying, raring, raying

7 Letter Words

angrily, jarring

8 Letter Words

9 Letter Words

jarringly

Words: 35

95

4 Letter Words

acre, care, cart, cera, cram, earn, emir, eric, erin, iran, mare, mart, mire, near, race, rain, rant, rate, ream, rein, rent, rica, rice, rien, rime, rite, tare, tear, term, tern, tier, tire, tram, trim

5 Letter Words

artem, cairn, caret, carne, carte, cater, certi, crane, crate, cream, crime, erica, icier, inert, inter, intra, irate, marie, mater, merit, miner, nacre, nicer, ramie, react, recta, recti, remit, rican, tamer, timer, trace, train, trice, trine

6 Letter Words

airmen, antrim, canter, carnet, cretan, cretin, crime, crimen, maitre, marine, mariti, marten, martin, mercat, metric, mincer, minter, nectar, nitric, recant, remain, retain, retina, tinier, trance

7 Letter Words

airtime, carmine, certain, crimean, crimina, incerta, inciter, inertia, interim, martini, mercati, mercian, minaret, raiment, termini

8 Letter Words

9 Letter Words

criminate

Words: 110

96

4 Letter Words

cues, cuss, icus, june, sues, suns, uses

5 Letter Words

issue, jesus, juice, junes, secus, sinus

6 Letter Words

census, juices

7 Letter Words

cuisine

8 Letter Words

9 Letter Words

juiciness

Words: 17

Solutions

97

4 Letter Words

dale	dare	dart	date	deal	dear	deer	doer	dole
dolt	dora	dote	drat	lade	lard	lead	load	lode
lord	read	redo	reed	road	rode	teed	toad	toed
told	trod							

5 Letter Words

adler	adore	alder	dealt	delta	deter	dotal
eared	elder	erode	oared	older	rated	toted
trade	tread	treed				

6 Letter Words

dealer	elated	leader	loader	lotted	orated
ordeal	ratted	reload	retold	rotted	tetrad

7 Letter Words

alerted	altered	delator	leotard	rattled	treated
related	rotated	totaled	treadle		

8 Letter Words

9 Letter Words

tolerated

98

Words: 69

4 Letter Words

coif	coin	fins	fisc	foci	icon	icus	info
ions	ious	sufi					

5 Letter Words

coifs	coins	conic	icons	scion	sonic
sufic	unius				

6 Letter Words

cousin	fusion

7 Letter Words

8 Letter Words

9 Letter Words

confucius

Words: 22

99

4 Letter Words

glue	lrun	lung	lure	rule	rune	rung	ugly
urge	your	yule					

5 Letter Words

gluey	gluon	gruel	lunge	rogue	rouen
rouge	young			

6 Letter Words

eulogy	gurney	lounge

7 Letter Words

lounger	urology	younger

8 Letter Words

9 Letter Words

neurology

Words: 26

100

4 Letter Words

alto	atom	into	iota	iron	limo	lion	loam	loan
loin	loma	lori	malo	moan	moat	moil	molt	morn
mort	mota	nato	noir	norm	nota	olin	oman	omit
oral	riot	roam	roan	roil	rota	taro	toil	torn
trio								

5 Letter Words

aaron	alamo	amino	animo	aorta	aroma	intol
intro	loran	manor	maori	mario	minor	molar
moral	omnia	ratio	roman	talon	timor	tirol
tonal						

6 Letter Words

amoral	aortal	atonal	latino	marino	marion
matron	mortal	normal	oilman	ration	rialto
romana	tailor				

7 Letter Words

laotian	romania

8 Letter Words

animator	manorial	notarial	rational

9 Letter Words

laminator

Words: 80

Solutions

101

4 Letter Words — Words: 41

alto avon loan lout lyon nato nota nova
only oral oval roan rota rout taro tony
torn tory tour troy tyro unto volt your

5 Letter Words

loran ovary rayon royal talon tonal
tyrol valor volta

6 Letter Words

layout notary outlay outran ovular
taylor votary

7 Letter Words

8 Letter Words

9 Letter Words

voluntary

102

4 Letter Words — Words: 30

evil levi live love move sive veil vies
vile viol vole

5 Letter Words

elvis evils ivies lives loves moves
movie olive solve veils viols voile
voles

6 Letter Words

movies olives pelvis voiles

7 Letter Words

plosive

8 Letter Words

9 Letter Words

implosive

103

4 Letter Words — Words: 82

amps apes apse asps camp cape caps ceps comp
cope cops epos maps mope mops nape naps neap
opec open pace pane pans paso pass peas pens
peon peso poem pose saps snap soap sops span
spas spec

5 Letter Words

aesop apses aspen camps capes capon comps
copes copse epsom epson mopes napes neaps
opens paces panes pecan pensa peons pesos
poems poses posse scamp scope snaps soaps
space spans spasm specs

6 Letter Words

aspens capons copses encamp pecans scamps
scopes spaces

7 Letter Words

compass copeman encamps

8 Letter Words

9 Letter Words

encompass

104

4 Letter Words — Words: 35

acne acre cage cane care cera cere cone
core corn crag cure ecru once race

5 Letter Words

acorn canoe cargo carne conga crane
crone curae grace nacre ocean ounce

6 Letter Words

careen conger cornea cougar encore

7 Letter Words

cornage courage

8 Letter Words

9 Letter Words

encourage

Solutions

105

Words: 151

4 Letter Words

alts, ante, ants, arts, arty, east, eats, etna, last, late, leet, lent, lest, lets, neat, nest, nets, rant, rate, rats, rent, rest, salt, sale, seat, sent, seta, slat, stan, star, stay, tale, tans, tare, tars, teal, tear, teas, teen, tees, tens, tern, tray, tree, trey

5 Letter Words

alert, alter, antes, aster, eaten, eater, elate, enter, entry, ernst, ester, later, leant, least, leets, nasty, rants, rates, rents, resat, reset, salty, satyr, setae, slant, slate, sleet, stale, stare, steal, steel, steer, stele, stern, stray, style, tales, tansy, tares, teals, tears, teary, tease, teens, teeny, tense, terns, terse, trays, trees, treys, tyler, yeast, yenta

6 Letter Words

alerts, alters, antler, astern, easter, eaters, eatery, elates, enters, estray, lateen, learnt, neater, neatly, nester, nestle, realty, relate, relent, rental, resent, sateen, senate, sentry, sleety, staler, steely, sterna, teasel, teaser, teensy, tenser, yentas

7 Letter Words

antlers, earnest, eastern, eternal, lateens, leanest, nearest, realest, relates, relents, rentals, stanley, stealer, sternly, styrene, tensely, tersely

8 Letter Words

easterly

9 Letter Words

earnestly

106

Words: 180

4 Letter Words

aces, acme, ails, aims, alec, ales, alms, alps, amps, apes, apis, apse, asps, calm, came, camp, cams, cape, caps, case, clam, clap, ilea, ipsa, lace, laic, lame, lamp, lams, laps, lass, leap, leas, lima, lisa, mace, macs, maes, mail, male, mali, maps, mass, meal, mesa, mica, pace, pail, pais, pale, palm, pals, pass, peal, peas, pica, pisa, plea, sacs, sail, sale, same, saps, scam, seal, seam, seas, siam, slam, slap, spas

5 Letter Words

aisle, alice, amies, amiss, ample, apses, aspic, calms, camel, camps, capes, cases, celia, claim, clamp, clams, claps, clasp, class, elias, emacs, ileac, islam, laces, lames, lamps, lapis, lapse, leaps, lessa, limas, maces, mails, males, maple, masse, meals, mesas, micas, paces, pails, pales, palms, peals, picas, place, pleas, psalm, sails, salem, sales, salic, salmi, scale, scalp, scamp, scams, seals, seams, sepal, sepia, sisal, slams, slaps, space, spasm

6 Letter Words

aisles, apices, aspics, camels, claims, clamps, clasps, impale, lapses, lassie, lipase, malice, maples, mescal, missal, passim, piacle, places, plaice, psalms, salmis, sample, scales, scalps, scampi, scamps, sepals, sepias, spaces

7 Letter Words

aimless, impales, impasse, melissa, mescals, palsies, piacles, plaices, samples, special

8 Letter Words

escapism, misplace, specials

9 Letter Words

misplaces

107

Words: 100

4 Letter Words

ails, ales, elks, fail, teal, file, flak, flan, flea, ilea, isle, kale, kiel, kiln, klan, lain, lake, lane, lank, lass, leaf, leak, lean, leas, leis, lens, less, lief, lien, lies, life, like, line, link, lisa, neil, nile, sail, sale, seal, self, silk, nail

5 Letter Words

aisle, alien, alike, ankle, elfin, elias, fails, false, falsi, files, final, flake, flank, flask, fleas, flies, isles, kilns, lakes, lanes, leafs, leaks, leans, lessa, liens, liken, likes, lines, links, nails, sails, sales, seals, silks, sisal, slain, slake, slink, snail

6 Letter Words

aisles, aliens, ankles, finale, finals, flakes, flanks, flasks, lassie, likens, saline, silken, slakes, slinks, snails

7 Letter Words

finales

8 Letter Words

sealskin

9 Letter Words

flakiness

108

Words: 7

4 Letter Words

vill, viol, volt

5 Letter Words

viols, volts

6 Letter Words

7 Letter Words

8 Letter Words

kilovolt

9 Letter Words

kilovolts

Solutions

109

4 Letter Words

celt, clef, feel, felt, file, flee, flit, leer, leet, left, lice, lief, life, lift, lire, lite, lyre, reel, refl, rely, rile, tile

5 Letter Words

cleft, creel, cyril, elect, elite, filer, filet, fleet, flier, flirt, flyer, leery, lefty, licet, lifer, liter, lyric, relic, rifle, tiler, tyler

6 Letter Words

celery, eerily, filter, fleecy, flirty, freely, lifter, relict, relief, trifle

7 Letter Words

erectly, fertile, reflect

8 Letter Words

celerity, fiercely

9 Letter Words

electrify

110

Words: 20

4 Letter Words

acta, cart, cram, curt, mica, rica, tact, uric

5 Letter Words

actum, amica, attic, carat, carta, curat, curia, tacit, tract, utica

6 Letter Words

tarmac

7 Letter Words

8 Letter Words

9 Letter Words

traumatic

111

Words: 61

4 Letter Words

adit, amid, arid, damn, darn, dart, dint, dirt, doit, doni, doom, door, dora, dorm, dram, drat, maid, mind, modi, mood, odor, raid, rand, rind, road, rood, toad, trod

5 Letter Words

admit, adorn, dinar, donor, drain, droit, mardi, monad, nadir, nomad, radio, radon, rondo, tondo, triad

6 Letter Words

adroit, diatom, domain, domino, indoor, inroad, nimrod, ordain, random

7 Letter Words

donatio, donator, doorman, doormat, dormant, mordant, tornado

8 Letter Words

tandoori

9 Letter Words

dominator

112

Words: 89

4 Letter Words

aced, aden, ands, cads, card, dace, dana, dane, dank, dare, dark, darn, dean, dear, deck, dens, desk, edna, ends, nerd, rand, read, reds, rend, sand, send

5 Letter Words

andes, arced, arden, asked, cadre, caked, caned, cards, cared, cased, cedar, daces, dakar, dance, danes, dares, darks, darns, deans, dears, decks, drake, drank, knead, naked, nerds, raced, raked, rands, rased, reads, rends, sedan

6 Letter Words

andrea, arcade, ascend, cadres, canard, cedars, craned, dancer, dances, danker, darken, decana, drakes, kneads, racked, ranked, sacked, sacred, sander, sandra, scared, snaked, snared

7 Letter Words

arcades, canards, cranked, dancers, darkens, snacked

8 Letter Words

9 Letter Words

ransacked

Solutions

113

4 Letter Words

ante	aver	earn	ears	ease	east	eats	eons	eras	eros	etna	eves	nave
near	neat	nero	nest	nets	noes	nose	note	ones	ores	oven	over	rase	rate	rave	reae
reno	rent	rest	revs	roes	rose	rote	rove	sane	sate	save	sean	sear	seat	seen	seer
sent	sera	sere	seta	sore	tare	tear	teas	teen	tees	tens	tern	toes	tone	tore	tree
vane	vase	veer	vent	vest	veto	vets	vote				

5 Letter Words

antes	arose	aster	atone	avers	avert	earns	eaten	eater	eaton	eaves	enter	erase
ernst	ester	evens	event	naves	nears	nerve	never	norse	notae	notes	novae	oaten
onere	onset	orate	ovate	ovens	overs	overt	rates	raven	raves	rents	resat	reset
rotes	roves	saner	saver	seato	serve	servo	setae	seven	sever	snare	sneer	snore
soave	stare	stave	steer	steno	stern	steve	stone	store	stove	tares	tears	tease
teens	tenor	tense	terns	terse	toner	tones	trees	trove	vanes	veers	vents	versa
verse	verso	voter	votes								

6 Letter Words

astern	atones	averse	averts	easter	eaters	enters	events	neater	nerves	nester
orates	ornate	ravens	reason	resent	revest	sateen	senate	starve	stereo	sterna
steven	strove	tavern	teaser	tenors	tenser	tensor	toners	troves	vaster	venter
vetoes	voters					

7 Letter Words

earnest	eastern	estover	nearest	nervosa	overate	overeat	roseate	senator
servant	taverns	treason	versant	veteran			

8 Letter Words

overeats	renovate	resonate	veterans

9 Letter Words

renovates

114

Words: 208

4 Letter Words

aces	acts	ansi	ants	asks	cans	case	cask	cast	cats	east	eats	ices	inks	kiss	kist
kits	nest	nets	nits	sack	sacs	sake	sane	sank	sans	sate	scan	scat	sean	seas	seat
sect	sent	seta	sets	sick	sine	sink	sins	site	sits	skin	skis	skit	snit	stan	tans
task	teas	tens	tics	ties	tins						

5 Letter Words

actes	anise	antes	antis	asset	cakes	canes	cants	cases	casks	caste	casts	cents
cista	cites	incas	inset	kites	knits	necks	nests	nicks	nikes	sacks	saint	sakes
oaten	sates	satin	scans	scant	scats	scent	scite	seats	sects	since	sinks	sitae	sites
reset	skate	skein	skies	skins	skits	snack	snake	sneak	snick	snits	stack	stain	stake
snore	stank	steak	stein	stick	sties	stink	tacks	takes	tanks	tasks	teaks	ticks	tikes
tease	tines										

6 Letter Words

anises	antics	ascent	assent	atkins	casein	casket	castes	enacts	incest	insect
insets	nicest	saints	sanest	sansei	satins	scants	scents	scites	secant	sicken
siesta	skates	skeins	snacks	snakes	sneaks	snicks	stacie	stacks	stains	stakes
stance	steaks	steins	sticks	stinks	tisane					

7 Letter Words

ascents	caskets	catkins	insects	intakes	seasick	secants	sestina	sickens
sickest	stances	tansies	tisanes				

8 Letter Words

snakiest

9 Letter Words

tackiness

115

Words: 97

4 Letter Words

ahem	amos	atom	dame	dams	dash	date	doha	ease
east	eats	edam	hams	hate	hats	head	heat	made
maes	mash	mast	mate	math	mats	mead	meat	mesa
moat	mota	oath	oats	same	sate	seam	seat	seta
shad	sham	shat	soda	soma	tads	tame	tams	team
teas	toad						

5 Letter Words

adeem	atoms	dames	dates	death	eadem	eased
edema	hades	haste	hated	hates	heads	heats
hosea	mated	mates	meats	moats	oaths	sated
seato	setae	shade	shame	shoat	stead	steam
stoma	tamed	tames	teams	tease	toads	

6 Letter Words

adeems	amsted	deaths	edemas	heated	mashed
seamed	seated	sedate	shamed	teamed	teased
thomas					

7 Letter Words

headset	steamed

8 Letter Words

9 Letter Words

homestead

116

Words: 46

4 Letter Words

ekes	eros	eyes	eyre	keys	ores	oyer	reek
rest	roes	rose	rote	ryes	seek	seer	sere
sore	tees	toes	tore	tree	trek	trey	yoke
yore							

5 Letter Words

esker	ester	eyres	oyers	reeks	reset
rotes	skeet	steer	stoke	store	terse
trees	treks	treys	yokes		

6 Letter Words

oyster	stereo	stoker	stroke

7 Letter Words

8 Letter Words

9 Letter Words

keystroke

Solutions

117

4 Letter Words

alit	aril	chit	cite	eire	eric	erie	hail	hair
heir	hilt	hire	ilea	ital	itch	laic	lair	liar
lice	lira	lire	lite	rail	rial	rica	rice	rich
rile	rite	tail	thai	tier	tile	tire		

5 Letter Words

alice	celia	certi	chair	chile	elite	erica
ethic	ileac	irate	licet	liter	lithe	recti
reich	relic	retie	riche	their	tiler	trail
trial	trice					

6 Letter Words

aliter	archie	claire	eclair	either	hailer
halite	hitler	lacier	litera	recite	relict
retail	thrice	tierce			

7 Letter Words

article   atelier   charlie   ethical   heretic
literae   recital

8 Letter Words

9 Letter Words

heretical

118

Words: 80

4 Letter Words

both	hill	hilt	hint	loth	thin

5 Letter Words

nihil

6 Letter Words

hilton

7 Letter Words

8 Letter Words

9 Letter Words

billionth

Words: 9

119

4 Letter Words

abel	able	bail	bale	bali	bane	bare	barn	bean
bear	beef	been	beer	bern	bier	bile	brae	bran
brie	elba	elbe	flab					

5 Letter Words

abler	baler	belie	bilan	blare	blear	brain
brian	brief	brine	faber	fable	fiber	liber
libra	libre	rebel				

6 Letter Words

bailee	bailer	baleen	beanie	belief	berlin
bernie	enable				

7 Letter Words

febrile   finable   friable

8 Letter Words

fineable

9 Letter Words

inferable

120

4 Letter Words

buds	bums	buns	doun	dubs	dues	dumb	dune	duns
duos	emus	menu	moue	mums	muse	nubs	nude	numb
onus	snub	sued	sumo	unde	undo	used		

Words: 57

5 Letter Words

bonum	bonus	bosun	bound	domus	douns	douse
dunes	menus	modus	moues	mound	mouse	mumbo
mused	nudes	numbs	sebum	sedum	sound	

6 Letter Words

bounds	buenos	bummed	busmen	mounds	moused
numbed	summed	summon	undoes		

7 Letter Words

8 Letter Words

summoned

9 Letter Words

ombudsmen

We hope you loved the logic puzzles. If you did, would you consider posting an online review?

This helps us to continue providing great products, and helps potential buyers to make confident decisions.

For more logic puzzles, find our similar titles

www.ingramcontent.com/pod-product-compliance
Lightning Source LLC
Chambersburg PA
CBHW081334080526
44588CB00017B/2625